ASTONISHED

ALSO BY BEVERLY DONOFRIO

✦

Riding in Cars with Boys

Looking for Mary

ASTONISHED

A Story of Evil,
Blessings, Grace,
and Solace

Beverly Donofrio

VIKING

VIKING
Published by the Penguin Group
Penguin Group (USA) Inc., 375 Hudson Street,
New York, New York 10014, U.S.A.
Penguin Group (Canada), 90 Eglinton Avenue East, Suite 700,
Toronto, Ontario, Canada M4P 2Y3
(a division of Pearson Penguin Canada Inc.)
Penguin Books Ltd, 80 Strand, London WC2R 0RL, England
Penguin Ireland, 25 St. Stephen's Green, Dublin 2, Ireland
(a division of Penguin Books Ltd)
Penguin Group (Australia), 707 Collins Street, Melbourne, Victoria 3008
Australia (a division of Pearson Australia Group Pty Ltd)
Penguin Books India Pvt Ltd, 11 Community Centre,
Panchsheel Park, New Delhi–110 017, India
Penguin Group (NZ), 67 Apollo Drive, Rosedale, Auckland 0632,
New Zealand (a division of Pearson New Zealand Ltd)
Penguin Books (South Africa), Rosebank Office Park, 181 Jan Smuts Avenue,
Parktown North 2193, South Africa
Penguin China, B7 Jiaming Center, 27 East Third Ring Road North,
Chaoyang District, Beijing 100020, China

Penguin Books Ltd, Registered Offices: 80 Strand, London WC2R 0RL, England

First published in 2013 by Viking Penguin, a member of Penguin Group (USA) Inc.

1 3 5 7 9 10 8 6 4 2

"New Year's Resolution" from *Blue Music: Poems* by Albert W. Starkey.
Copyright © 2012 by Albert W. Starkey. Reprinted by permission of the author.

LIBRARY OF CONGRESS CATALOGING IN PUBLICATION DATA
Donofrio, Beverly.
Astonished : a story of evil, blessings, grace, and solace / Beverly Donofrio.
pages cm
ISBN 978-0-670-02575-6
1. Donofrio, Beverly. 2. Catholics—Biography. 3. Rape victims—Religious life.
4. Rape—Religious aspects—Christianity. 5. Christian pilgrims and pilgrimages—
Mexico. 6. Monasteries—Mexico. I. Title.
BX4705.D6146A3 2013
818'.5403—dc23
[B]   2012039753

Printed in the United States of America
Set in Aldus LT Std
Designed by Francesca Belanger

*Penguin is committed to publishing works of quality and integrity.
In that spirit, we are proud to offer this book to our readers;
however, the story, the experiences, and the words
are the author's alone.*

For Suzy, Connie, and Eric

New Year's Resolution

Is the suffering
A howl of the animal to survive
Or an ache of the soul to thrive?
I'm afraid so.
There is no way out of this
Only a way in, to where
The animal soul is breathing
For someone who is not afraid
To stare life in the face
And stop looking for answers
To sunsets, tides, and seasons.

Albert W. Starkey

We accept good things from God
And should we not accept evil?

Job

Contents

ASTONISHED

Disrupted

Even though I do know the important question is not why this happened to me but what I'm going to do now; and even though I was fifty-five and the attacker was a serial rapist in a small town, raping gringo women between fifty and sixty; and even though I, along with the entire town, felt like evil had come for a visit and it was not personal; and even though this little round-faced pervert with a big-billed baseball cap woke me in the middle of the night in the middle of a deep sleep in my own bed with a knife inches from my face, I was absolutely shocked that he chose *me*. This was *not* supposed to happen; I was supposed to have escaped: I had hot flashes and liver spots and was finally in the final stretch. I'd survived all these decades without experiencing this thing I dreaded as much as death—and had just been looking for a *monastery* to join, for Christ's sake.

Why now? I'd lived for thirteen years in New York City, eleven of them in Alphabet City, back when there was a crack house on every other block and storefronts where everyone and his brother came to slip five bucks under a glass window to purchase little baggies of pot, a fix of heroin, a toot of cocaine. Back then there was a roach exterminator's office on the ground floor of my building, where you can now buy green smoothies and wheatgrass shots. The neighborhood was crawling with, excuse my judgment, *lowlifes*, who all knew I lived alone with my twelve-year-old son.

I couldn't walk from my building to the corner to get a carton of milk without some guy or three or four making a crack, "Mmmm, mama, take me home wit you," or even more annoyingly, *tsk-tsking* his tongue as though he were enticing a cat. Standing in crowded subway cars men jammed knees between my legs, pressed hard-ons against my butt, tongues wiggled lasciviously; across the aisle a man in a coat opened his legs to flash me. Alone in a movie theater I was a magnet for creeps to jerk off beside.

The first words I ever published, in *The New York Times*, in the "Metropolitan Diary," told how I was waiting for the light to change at First Avenue and St. Mark's Place, when a man came up and said, "Hi, remember me? I'm the guy who told you you had nice legs over on Fourteenth Street."

Really?

The second year I lived in New York, in 1979, I moved into a loft on Broadway between Prince and Spring with my boyfriend. One night I stood in the street doorway, my key in the lock, when a guy shoved up against me, panting. "Give me your money." I had five dollars in my pocket, which I handed over.

"Is that all?" he said.

"Yes." It was the truth.

"Your husband home?"

"He's upstairs," I lied, then he pinched my crotch and ran off.

The boyfriend and I didn't last, and I moved to the East Village, where one night, soon after the move, I was walking down St. Mark's Place alone at four in the morning.

If I was going to be raped, why didn't it happen then? I prided myself on being fearless, but I was virtually never cautious or even careful.

One of the other stragglers on St. Mark's rushed up from behind and grabbed me, pinning my arms to my sides, his breath high in his chest. "I got you! You're coming with me."

It was as though some motherly, emergency-room-nurse creature zoomed into me. "Calm down. Look at the water," I said. It was streaming in the gutter from an opened fire hydrant. "It's okay." I slipped out my arm and rubbed his back. "You're okay. What's your name?"

"Snake."

"Your name's not Snake."

He breathed out "Bobbie," and I knew I was safe. When we reached the corner he asked for a dollar to buy a cup of coffee, and I gave him a quarter.

Then one day the tide clearly began to turn. I was thirty-six. It was a Sunday in winter, and I was walking on my block down Avenue A. My hair was black, but I'd begun getting gray hair when I was twelve and by now had a full head of salt and pepper, wishing for a nice hunk of white to grow in front and make me look like Cruella de Vil. So, this day, on the other side of the street a guy calls, "Hey, lady, green legs don't go with gray hair." I was insulted. Green tights *did* go with gray hair, and I fully intended to wear green tights until I died.

A few years before this, a friend and I walked 110 blocks from Columbia University to my place on Twelfth Street and Avenue A, and four, no exaggeration, *four* men exposed themselves to us. Once when I was a typist, sitting in a pool of secretaries outside the doors of the offices where all the men worked, I received an obscene phone call. He murmured, all breathy, "You know what I want to do to you . . . ," and I said, "Excuse me, is this an obscene phone call? Hold on, let me put you on speakerphone." Naturally, he hung up.

In my hometown, I was signing books after a reading in the basement of Holy Trinity Church. A woman came up and said,

"Oh, Bev, the things those boys used to say to you. Remember? Fifth-grade catechism?"

I did not remember anything except their calling me up to blurt on the phone, "Knockers, headlights, bazoombas, brassiere." I had the great misfortune of developing breasts early. But my breasts never developed into much, which would not account for my continuing to be such a target for the wrong kind of male attention.

I'm sure I was far from the only girl enduring such humiliations, but I still wondered: Is there something about me?

This was not a new question. And this old question did not go flashing through my mind as I looked at the rapist's knife in my face.

What went flashing through my mind was *Now I'm going to be raped. Now, God?* Followed by the heart of the matter, *I can't believe You! You sent a rapist to my bed? To me, who doesn't let a day go by without talking to, without contemplating, You?*

The next thought almost did me in: I do not want to believe in a God that would let this happen. If I lose God, if I don't believe in God anymore, I won't be able to find meaning in an alarming event, in every synchronicity; have no more sense of a love flowing everywhere; no more feeling of a warm embracing presence; no more belief that there's a light in the center of you and me, a light that can grow peace in the world; no more waking in the night and comforting myself back to sleep like a lullaby, with *Hail Marys*; no more hope of grace coming to the rescue.

And then there was the very disturbing matter of never, ever being the same person who'd gone innocently, trustingly, to sleep that night.

Not ever again.

I was the house of cards falling to the floor. I was the seed sown in choking weeds. The fig tree that didn't produce.

Seven years before the rape:

The Virgin Mary, whom I consider a feminine manifestation of God, called me into a white-hot conversion, a change of life in the middle of a change of life. Mary was a kiss on the top of my head, the sun in my heart, the love with which I loved her. Nothing was the same. I even upped and moved to Mexico because they parade her through the streets on pallets there. They play her song, *Ave Maria*, at noon. She floats above altars while church bells ring so loudly they turn your head.

God is alive and well in Mexico, I told people back home. I think they thought I was nuts.

God was alive and well for a year or two. And then getting and spending, a busy social life, building a house—all the consuming details that crowd the space in one's daily life—dimmed the intensity of my conversion experience, and God began to fade like fabric in the sun. At the time, I had no awareness of a faith journey's ups and downs—or that the first phase had ended and a new stage had begun.

I built a bright airy house in Mexico in the old colonial town San Miguel de Allende and planted an *ojo de pollo* at the base of an ochre column in my garden. Its vines of bright yellow flowers with brown eyes climbed bushy and heavy all the way to the ceiling of my second-floor terrace and were headed to the roof. I never believed I could ever afford to own a house, and the robustness of the plant seemed a physical manifestation of the trajectory my life had taken since I moved to my adopted country.

I'd bought the potted plant two years before on February

2nd, Candelaria in Spanish and Candlemass in English, which celebrates Christ as the light of the world. For some reason, in Mexico women and girls carry their baby Jesus dolls around town that day then place them at the foot of the altar for a priest to bless after mass with holy water. I did not own a baby Jesus doll but I now owned an *ojo de pollo*, and walking home through the streets with it, I was filled with love and awe for a town where women and children cradled Jesus dolls as though they were real, adored and cared for God in the form of a helpless infant. I wanted the culture of this town, where belief was so innocent and strong it animated symbols, to rub off on me, I wanted to live under the skin of this place, and I wanted my plant in the earth and not in its pot so I'd be able to take it with me the next time I moved.

I'd no idea how I could swing buying land and building a house, but one day I called a phone number I'd seen painted like graffiti next to *Se Vende* on a crumbling brick wall near my rental. When the owner opened the rusted gate, I saw a narrow weedy field in the middle of which a pineapple palm held out its arms to me. I summoned the nerve to ask to borrow money from friends, and in a month or so the property was mine. I designed the house so that when you opened the front door, the pineapple palm was the first thing you'd see at the end of the wide entryway, in the middle of the garden. You might also notice St. Francis near the palm, under which I planned to bury my beloved cat Cyrano.

The back of the house faces a canyon, but the front is on a busy street near centro, which meant I was near enough to town to walk everywhere. Early mornings I'd hear a rooster crow on my way to yoga down Calle Animas following a stream of people who'd just debarked a bus from the campo. On my way home from Yoga I might stop for a cappuccino or breakfast with friends at an outdoor café; or if it were a day my maid, Lupe, worked, I'd buy homemade tortillas from a woman sitting on the steps in Plaza Civica, and Lupe would make me quesadillas or an onion omelet then serve it to me with her delicious salsa, a napkin, and limonada on the terrace next to the *ojo de pollo*. After breakfast I'd bring out my laptop and work until the sun grew too bright, and then I'd move to my office.

Days were for writing and nights were for dinners, drinks, concerts, art openings, readings. I was very busy in my adopted town. I learned to salsa and paint icons. I raised money for charitable causes. Sometimes there weren't enough nights in the week to fit in all my interesting friends, and new friends arrived every winter and summer season. I gave a dance party once, and we shook the house. Instead of making our arms spell out YMCA, we spelled out AARP.

I even became engaged to a performance artist. I first laid eyes on him when during the curtain call of a play staged in a boxing rink, the director motioned to the light booth high above where Pepe Filipe (not his real name) removed his beret and humbly bowed. The corkscrews in his ponytail flounced, the diamond in his ear glinted, and his tie-dyed t-shirt with the sleeves cut off revealed sleekly muscled arms with a tattoo on each shoulder. I knew him. He was something dark, an outcast, bohemian, anarchist who'd seen too much of the world. He was obviously handy: he could light a stage, which I extrapolated to include build a house, fix cars, read a woman like a book and play her like a violin. It wasn't every day or every year, or more than twice in the last decade, for that matter, that I encountered a man who could shake me out of my celibate stupor strongly enough to make me take notice. My gut not only reacted, it talked to me. It said, This man can fly you to the moon.

Why could I never settle for Cincinnati?

He slipped love poems into my palm in public and wrote love notes on my bathroom mirror. We'd been together six weeks when, watching the Twin Towers fall, we exclaimed (could it really have been?), simultaneously, "Let's get married." He wanted to buy a van and drive around the country putting on shows with me as his assistant. In one act I would wear a leotard and stand stiff as a board pretending to be a bass while he played jazz on me. I actually considered this.

The night the relationship ended, he held a knife over his head and wailed to the heavens, "I can't *take it anymore!*" He was of Spanish descent. My heart did not break, but I did shave my head to let my hair grow in gray in the hope that looking more mature would make me be so.

I had fun at parties, drank margaritas at sunset, ran a lecture series, wrote, taught writing workshops, wore big spangly necklaces, bright lipstick, a silk *rebozo* draped on my shoulder. And the few times a man did appear, I warded him off at the pass. My life was busy with people. Still I was lonely with a loneliness no man, friend, or activity had ever filled.

But not long ago, Mary had.

I still prayed *Hail Marys*, even in Spanish. I prayed the Jesus prayer. I sat in silence. I read Buddhist books, went to Yogananda services, practiced many meditation techniques. I breathed in suffering and breathed out peace. I breathed in cruelty and breathed out loving-kindness. I imagined my heart opened like a lotus. I spread love in expanding waves to my neighbors, my street, my town, my country, the continent, the world, solar system, Milky Way, universe. I missed God. I kept very busy. I felt alone.

And then arrived: Zachary Brewer Donofrio, my grandbaby, son of my son. A common miracle not common at all. My ear to his

bud of a heart. My nose to his new-leaf skin. Boneless toes between my lips. His sleeping body on my body rising and falling
with my breath. My heart opened like a lotus. Love expanded in
waves that rippled to the edge of the universe. I breathed him in;
I breathed out peace.

When I left him in Brooklyn, saying goodbye was a wound
in my side, a cross to bear.

Back in Mexico, a country away from new love, my old, for-
merly interesting life felt as exciting as a flat line. Worse: it felt
frivolous. Compared to the bright possibility of my grandson's
new life, my fifty-five years on the planet seemed a whole lot of
potential spoiled to a stink. My heart so unaccustomed to feeling
such love had been shocked into a stupor. I awoke every night in
agony, prodding a pitchfork at my own self: old, unlovable, un-
loved, incapable of—you name it. Worthless, failed, wrong
choices, wrong wrong wrong, almost dead, no more time, no
more hope, no more use of even trying. No more appetite for,
well, anything this life had to dish up anyway. St. John of the
Cross might have called it a Dark Night of the Soul; I called it a
depression. I did not keep very busy. I felt no joy. I missed God. I
was very alone.

Every memory, thought, reflection was bruised black and blue.
Every day gray as fog. I refused invitations, dreaded public gatherings, slithered around the backstreets of town to avoid even
my friends. Somewhere, somehow, I'd lost myself, and this realization began creeping in: it had happened before my grandson's
arrival.

I did sometimes hike up the mountain to the botanical preserve in the hope that increasing my heart rate might increase
something else, too: an appetite for this life. I prayed most of the

way, the usual memorized prayers—the Rosary, *Hail Marys*, *Hail Holy Queens*, *Our Fathers*, *Memorares*, chanting them really, like a prisoner on a chain gang—without ever once managing a single sincere plea, a down-on-my-knees beg to God for help. That kind of prayer would have required a faith I did not want to chance finding out had gone missing.

Once near sunset I remembered to sit in the middle of the dam that crossed the reservoir up there. If you did that at the right moment, a flock of ibises would fly ten feet above your head, taking off on their nightly migration back to the south side of town. I saw the black flock swarming low in the sky beyond the reservoir's shore and tilted my face up as they approached. Holding my breath under the mighty collective whirring fan of their wings, I felt the rushing breeze on my face, the ruffling of my hair, my shirt. The ibises had never failed to trigger my heart, make me smile. Now instead of fluttering against my ribs, my heart beat like it was slogging through quicksand.

Something was seriously wrong with me.

I was not much improved four months later when I returned to Brooklyn to visit Zach for a few weeks. In the middle of this stay, I needed some solitary time to meet a writing deadline and had an idea to write at a monastery I'd heard about on NPR years ago—the Abbey of Regina Laudis. I found it on the Internet and read that forty-five nuns in full habit run a farm in Bethlehem, Connecticut, and that they worship in Latin.

I wrote and promptly received an invitation to spend two days and two evenings. I borrowed my son's car, headed north, and found myself exiting the highway in a springtime Connecticut that actually smelled green. I followed the signs to the monastery and turned up a long, curved driveway where a nun drove by in a pickup, a sweatband over her wimple, and my heart did a cha cha that shook my world: That could be *me*. This could be the answer to a question I hadn't asked—yet. Observing ancient practices in a speeding world would make it slow down and, surely, give it the deeper meaning I was craving. I'd be very busy, milking cows, planting rows, chanting. The quotidian and the spiritual, the mundane and the sacred—there'd be no more separation.

Here I witnessed in action women living a life that until that moment I had only secretly fantasized about. They work a six-hundred-acre farm, are smithies, potters, cheese-makers, painters, strong capable women who gather throughout the day—and again at two every morning—to pray for the poor, the lonely, the lost, believing their prayers can lift us all up and heal the world. In a monastery, work is a form of prayer. What would that feel like? Devoting every moment, action, and thought to God could shift the focus from myself to something higher, sacred, mysterious, transcendent.

On my second and last day at the monastery, the sisters celebrated a feast day. Everyone in chapel—a few other retreatants, some townspeople, and I—were invited to join a procession. We gathered in the lobby and each was handed a relic to hold against our chests as we walked. Mine was a relic of a woman saint, which appeared to be a piece of fabric faded to no color, pinned to a chartreuse velvet background, under glass, inside a gold-leafed frame, the size of letter paper. The sisters led the way. The leader, a middle-aged nun with fair, unlined skin, held what appeared to be a very large Bible, almost the size of an atlas but thicker, arms straight, over her head. I was impressed by her strength, which could be the natural result of being a farmer.

We walked in silence down a path dappled with sunlight, winding through the woods into the cloistered area normally off limits to anyone but the nuns. Their black veils stirred in the breeze, their skirts billowed behind, and my heart filled with awe that this ancient ritual was still performed, and that I was part of it. Time slowed and I heard the birds, which had probably been chirping all along, and in the distance a cow lowing. I pressed the back of the relic to my chest and felt my heart beating against it and wondered how old this saint was when she died and if this fabric came from the dress she'd been wearing at the time. I wondered if she was tortured in some hideous martyred way because she refused to denounce her faith.

When I returned to the retreat house, on the floor of my bedroom, I found three pennies and remembered my mother saying whenever she found one, "Pennies from Heaven." And I interpreted them as a sign: crumbs on the path leading me to God. Failed ambitions, spoiled potential were no more important here than a thought you had yesterday and then forgot. To be silent, to pray ceaselessly, and never climb a ladder anywhere except literally to reach an object too high off the ground were as appealing to me as being admired by others used to be. Love is what would matter—for the rest of my life. I would love Jesus Christ, not only his Mother. I'd lose my life so I could gain it. I'd leave my life at a mature age, like sadhus in India do, and walk the path of enlightenment.

I already believed that God is love and that the more you love, the more love there is, and the less power evil has. Since Zach's birth I'd been acutely aware of how I'd closed myself off from love and had been avoiding the pain of living fully. But as a nun/monk I'd make of my life a total act of love. As a nun/monk I wouldn't feel so lonely. The lack of human love in my life I'd come to feel at the birth of Zachary would be subsumed by a larger love—for God, and for the whole world.

Back in Brooklyn I told my son how attracted I'd been to the monastery and wondered what he thought about the possibility of my joining a place where I'd be cloistered—where he could visit me but I'd rarely be able to visit him. "It would be in a beautiful place," I said, trying to ease the blow. He reached his hand to the counter to steady himself. "You know I'll feel abandoned," he said. "You won't see Zach graduate. You won't go to his wedding."

Jason is the only child of a mother who virtually never played with dolls, and then got pregnant as a teenager. When my teenage husband confessed he was a junkie, I divorced him, and by nineteen, I was a single mother without a car in a town without day care. I felt trapped in a life I didn't want, and I did not accept my limitations graciously. I blamed them on motherhood and could not wait to be liberated from it—when my son finally grew up. Meanwhile, I told him that we were a team—more like brother and sister than mother and son, we used to say. This was my philosophy: If I'm happy, my kid will be happy, so good childrearing be damned, it's more important I have fun. It was the late sixties and early seventies. I had sex with strangers, whom my son was forced to face on the mornings after. I did drugs that could kill a horse, hitchhiked, shoplifted, and dropped LSD with Jason in tow.

With some (late) maturity came a mother lode of sadness and guilt about how much I'd hurt my son, all the love I didn't give and the love I didn't claim. But Zachary had provided a bridge back to it. Looking into Zach's eyes as I fed him a bottle, I remembered how Jase and I gazed endlessly into each other's eyes, too, how when I fed him, I'd feather touch his fingers around the bottle and how with his other hand he'd be pulling my earlobe. I remembered how much I did love my baby. How I flew him on my shins through long lonely afternoons listening to *Sergeant Pepper*; how for longer than with anyone else in my life, he'd been my main companion.

When Jason entered therapy in his early twenties and began to truly face the neglect, the deprivations, the abuse, he could barely stand to be in my presence let alone speak to me. It was one of the reasons I'd found the Blessed Mother, to teach me to mother, and to somehow ease the guilt and depression that was crippling me. I prayed like my life depended on it, Jason and I talked about his feelings, I apologized, we went to therapy a few times, and he forgave me. Or tries to, over and over again.

With Zachary I'd been given a second chance, an answered prayer. I can nurture my grandson in a way I had not been capable of nurturing my son, and helping with Zachary meant helping my son, and being a good mother to him.

I wouldn't desert Jason; I wouldn't desert Zach. I thought how Christ said, "If you want to gain your life you must lose it." But he also said that the greatest commandments were to love God with all our hearts and souls and to love our neighbors as ourselves. Certainly "neighbor" must extend to family. Surely, I'd be able to find some contemplative monastery somewhere that would make an exception for me.

The way was clear. I was fifty-five years old now, I'd given up men, I was a member of the Catholic Church. I had no debt, ten thousand dollars in the bank, my cat of seventeen years had died the year before, I could easily sublet my house. The time was now. I'd make an itinerary; I'd spend every penny. I'd visit and I'd visit. And if it was God who'd lit this desire in me, God would light the way.

Back in Mexico again, certain I'd experienced a "call," I bookmarked, I jotted down notes, phone numbers, I spent hours, days, two weeks straight glued to my computer, hunting the net for a contemplative monastery to join. I was too excited, and obsessed, to be depressed. This is when, on June 22, two weeks after I'd begun the monastery search, I force myself at midnight to stop looking at pictures and reading charism statements, fold my laptop, turn off the light, and fall asleep. I do not take notice that it is John the Baptizer's day—when in Mexico they believe the rains come, blessedly ending the long seasonal drought, greening the world back to new life. It is the first hour of this day—at one in the morning—that the rapist chooses to wake me up, invade my life, slither into my bed, his body radiating heat inches from mine, the blade of his knife glinting in front of my face.

> The thing I have feared most
> is come up on me.
>
> Job

I know exactly who he is: our town's serial rapist, the one we haven't been able to catch. For eight months he's scaled walls, lassoed balconies, picked locks, removed skylights, cut glass from windows, and attacked four women, and with the exception of one, all over fifty. And each time, in a sick perversion of postcoital intimacy, he had the self-absorption to complain about how sick he is—in perfect accented English—looking for *sympathy*! And killing time until he could get it up for another round.

The first two women fought, so he beat them. The next two, hearing about the first two, didn't fight and escaped relatively unharmed if you can ever call being raped repeatedly unharmed. He returned to one of them a month after he attacked her. When she woke to the sound of cutting glass, and screamed, the rapist said, "It's okay, Margarita. It's only me."

If the town had a skin it would be covered with shingles, an agonizing rash of the nerves you can't for a second ignore. We'd imagined the rapist in every shadow, around every corner, he's in your house, under your bed, behind the clothes in your closet. He's peeping from your garden. The rapist is a one-man terrorist waiting to spring, and we've been on red alert for so long, people have fled town, put their houses up for sale, installed spotlights, alarm systems, bars on windows like prison cells. They've Googled recipes for pepper spray and mail-ordered mace. One friend locks herself in her bedroom every night and pees in a makeshift potty.

I'd spoken to the ex–FBI agent turned writer who'd retired to our town and was assisting the Mexican authorities. This is what she told me: Our class of serial rapist is the power-reassurance type. This means he has low self-esteem and needs victims to help him feel powerful. He harbors a deep-seated fantasy that his victims are his lovers, and if they fight, they enrage him. He's cunning and intelligent, stalks his victims, and plans meticulously like a socialite plans a thousand-dollar-a-seat dinner party.

He'd probably been in my house touching my things. He'd been sitting on the deserted hillside, watching me through my wall of windows: cooking, washing dishes, reading, undressing, searching for monasteries to join.

> In the experience of fear, Christians differ from
> nonbelievers . . .
> We may cry out that we are forsaken
> but the sense of being forsaken is part of the experience
> of the presence of God at such a time.
> That is how God is near.
>
> J. Neville Ward

A tug on the sheet, a sinking weight on the mattress, my body buzzes like a field of bees as my eyes fly open to the last thing I want to see. I do not look, but out of the corner of my eye, he is there, leaning on his elbow, his round face propped on his palm.

His big-billed baseball cap. He's made himself at home. He has appropriated me.

"Shshshshsh! Don't scream, I have a knife," he says, showing it to me, inches from my face. It's the long serrated one I'd sliced limes with and left on the counter. He couldn't bother to bring his own?

I am scared of being raped, of never forgiving God, of being ruined for life. I am not scared of the knife. I already know I will not fight and he will not cut me.

I am in a dank, dark ditch, and God is here, too, in the void of His absence.

The rapist moves in closer.

"Don't do this," I beg. "Please. It's not right. It's sick." He'd said those last five words himself to his other victims.

"Na, na, na," he imitates a baby, condescendingly. "You talk too much." He pounds my shoulder with the fist that holds the knife.

"I'm going to be sick," I lie. But as soon as I say it, it becomes the truth.

"Calm down. Look," he arcs the knife in the air. It lands on my altar next to the bed; I imagine its blade touching the white crushed-marble crucifix, my glow-in-the-dark Mary, my glow-in-the-dark rosary, a yellow candle in a painted tin holder shaped like a bleeding heart, pebbles and shells from places I have lived, a black-and-white-striped feather I found in the woods at the Abbey of Regina Laudis. Staring from the pomegranate wall behind us are the dozen Mary icons I painted. The icons I believed had the power to protect me.

"You want some wine?" he offers.

I refuse it. I keep my arms crossed over my chest. He does not kiss or touch. He smells of sour sweat and beer. His penis is the size of a woman's thumb. He finishes in two minutes.

And then he wants to talk. "Is your name Penelope? Are you *Inglaterra*? You married? I seen you on the street. You have a nice body."

I am filled with dread like a torture victim waiting in a cell. The rest of the night might not be so missionary. But I am not so afraid as before. It was good that his penis is an inch long and he finished in two minutes. It's enough I let him fuck me, I will *not* talk to him. I decide to ignore the whole scene and pray. As soon as I begin it occurs to me that I should pray out loud. I begin, *Hail Mary, full of grace*, and I am struck by a brilliant idea. I should pray in Spanish and freak the rapist out.

Dios te salve Maria.

"You're praying. Stop praying." He bangs my shoulder again.

"I'm praying for *you*." It's a lie I realize should be the truth. I pray a whole *Ave Maria* for him then almost finish a vehement *Padre Nuestro* before I realize I have never once since I woke up asked God to help me, yet I pray for help all the time. I pray for help when I have to meet someone I don't know very well for coffee. *Dios te salve Maria, llena eres de gracia*, please get him the hell out of my bed, *el señor es contigo*, please, God, Mary, Jesus, all you angels and saints, all you dead ancestors come and get him the hell out of my house, *bendita eres entre todas las mujeres*, he backs out of the bed, he zips his fly, *y bendita es el fruto de tu vientre, Jesus*, Mary, all you angels and saints, every dead relative, please make him leave, please make him leave, *Santa Maria, madre de dios*, get him out of my house; he sighs, "Okay," then says, "I'm going"; kisses me on the cheek, and backs out of bed, *ruega por nosotros pecadores*; "Goodbye," he says as he walks toward the door; *Ahora y la hora de nuestros muertos, amen.* "You'll be okay."

Go, go, go, keep going, "*Dios te salve Maria, llena eres—*" I begin again.

As though it's an afterthought, at the door he says, "Don't call the police." And then he leaves.

A few days after the rape, I will call a priest I know, crying, "Why would God do this?"

"God didn't do it."

"Then why did God allow it?"

"God doesn't cause evil. Ever. But God will use it."

What I didn't ask: "Well, who created the world and evil in it? And isn't God All-Powerful? Isn't He? Isn't He? Or is it She?" Really, though, I'm sure: God is an It.

Let me get this straight:

Evil paid me a visit.

Prayer chased it away.

Either God has no power to prevent evil, or God does have the power and allows or tolerates it anyway, uses evil to draw us back.

I can hear the rapist trot down the stairs, the front door open, then slam. I run down to lock it and listen to his footsteps walking quickly on the cobblestones, going around the corner. On my way back up the stairs, a dribble of sperm leaks onto my inner thigh, and I consider not reporting the rape. I consider the night ahead: the interrogation, medical exam, the humiliating details confessed to strangers. It's possible, I realize, not even to call the police. I don't want the whole town to know. I don't want to cause my son pain and worry. I don't want to go through the rest of my life known as a woman who'd been raped. A victim. How I've always despised being seen as a victim.

But before two minutes have passed, I understand that this isn't only about me. I have no choice. Women need to be warned. It had been months since the rapist's last attack, and we'd thought he might have left town. Women need to be vigilant again. Besides, I was a feminist, am a feminist. I could never look myself in the eye. So I do my duty and call.

The police arrive in trucks, on the backs of motorcycles, on horses.

My friends and neighbors, Caren and Dave, accompany me to the *Munesterio Publico*. After I've given my statement to a woman prosecutor, a strange, burly detective slides his chair in too close. "Tell me everything, leave out no details," he says.

"Read the report," I bark, sliding my chair away from his. "I'm not telling this over and over. It's too traumatic."

He rears back. I'd never seen a person turn literally dark before.

I am given a pelvic exam and submit to the taking of a digital photo—of my vagina, which the doctor shows to my friend Caren.

It's morning by the time I return to my house. A half-dozen detectives are still buzzing around. They brush for fingerprints, haul off bedding. A detective brings me onto the balcony outside my bedroom and points out a rope ladder hooked to my balcony rail.

I ask Caren to post a notice on the town's website that I've been raped.

The day after the rape, a social worker comes to my house. He is a young man who apologizes for what this man has done to me. I tell him I am fine. (And believe it.) I tell him how I prayed and the rapist left. I tell him it could have been much worse. He tells me that they counsel people dispatched to war to imagine the worst, most brutal horror they can muster. They do this so that when the worst, most brutal horror happens, it won't totally destroy them.

I had imagined being raped many times. Always worse than

what happened. I remain in shock. I now wonder if shock is a grace given by God.

I walk the streets, staring down every little barrel-like man I pass. Even though I never looked at his face, I am sure I will recognize the rapist when I see him. I am alarmed there are so many little barrel men; I am alarmed they're all staring at *me*. Had they always and I'd never noticed?

A shaman friend arrives. He drags my mattress onto the balcony, splashes it with *ruda* water, douses it with incense. He scatters bouquets of white lilies, daisies, carnations, spider mums on the platform where the mattress had lain. He burns candles there, too. He washes all the floors. He smudges every room. He spits water in my face then smudges me, too. Once he told me that his job is to fight evil. Now he clenches his fists, fills his chest with air, and says, "I'm gonna get the fucker."

A month later, after the shaman confesses that the evil had been so strong, he'd retched in my kitchen, I find a Bohemia beer the "fucker" left in the refrigerator door.

Once a famous psychic and Buddhist practitioner came to town. She has written books and counseled a president. She told me that evil is real and so is the devil. She told me the devil burned her apartment down. She told me that Jesus is incarnate and in Syria trying to save us from annihilating the world. She said she saw him dressed all in white at the side of a desert road. His eyes were blue as sapphires. She gave him a ride to a tent where they talked. Hmmm, I think. Maybe that's the Jesus I'll picture when I try, finally, to fall in love with him. Soon. At a monastery.

A priest does not come and sprinkle holy water. The only priest I know in the whole country is a cloistered Benedictine abbot with a monastery to run. It never occurs to ask him to leave the monastery and come to me.

I pray the St. Michael prayer, "Cast into hell Satan and all evil spirits who roam through the world seeking the ruin of souls." I pray, "Please God keep evil far away from me. Please God, Help, Protect, Heal." I believe God can and will keep evil away. I can't explain why I believe this, especially after what just happened to me. Maybe, because I so want to.

But all of me must not be convinced. I cannot fall asleep at night, because I'll be too vulnerable. I am afraid I will never sleep in the dark again. But I do have faith that soon, at a monastery, maybe I will find an oasis.

Now all of those worries and self-criticisms that used to keep me up, those pricks of the pitchfork, seem stupid and frivolous, ego-driven drivel. I want to pull down my ego, topple it like the statue of Saddam Hussein. It does not occur to me that this desire may be one of those ways God is using evil to help me.

> We are like people who hear snatches of music,
> which they have no means of relating
> to the symphony of the whole.
>
> Bede Griffiths

Until I was thirty, I had sex with men, many men, I didn't care about. Enjoyment was a bonus: rare. It was the 1960s into the '70s. The act was political; I had lots to prove.

Life was not a bed of roses, a bowl of cherries, a walk in the park. I was a single mother without a car when there were no day-care centers. I was evicted, twice; fired from jobs, twice; considered becoming a prostitute to pay for a dentist; I was arrested for possession of marijuana. All those mistakes, missteps, hard times, all those knocks made me tough, tough enough to survive this latest blow. I think: If it had to happen to someone, it's good it happened to me. I can take it. And God can use me.

My friends bring gifts and food. They cry and hug me. They cry and hug one another. It's a love-in at my house. Wyatt, eight years old, draws me a coat of arms in crayon that he sends to me through his mother. It has a lion's roaring face and under it: Beb [*sic*] the Courageous.

Nothing but the facts have been printed in the English-language newspaper so far. I begin to think the rapist picked me because God wanted me to help get him caught. Already, a few months before I was raped, hoping an NPR piece would spur the local authorities into action, I'd called NPR, which had then aired a story. It was followed by a piece in *The New York Times*. The town is dependent on tourism, and the bad publicity jolted it into gear: It hired more police, hired a liaison between the gringo and Mexican communities, held community meetings, established a hotline. The rapist had told two of his victims that he'd been in jail in the States, and rumors floated that the FBI was finally conducting DNA tests.

Before the rapist came to me, I'd been informed: I'd talked to two of his victims and to the ex–FBI agent consulting on the case. I'd possessed important information about the rapist's actions and his profile, an inside scoop that had helped me keep my head through the attack. I am a writer; I can be the messenger; I can share what I know.

In the article, I write everything I knew beforehand and everything that happened to me. And this is how it ends: "The outpouring of love and concern from both foreign and Mexican communities has been heartening and healing. I have always heard that we are all one. I never quite understood it the way I do now. Each time I'd heard how a woman among us had been raped I felt sick and outraged. Now, I am the one who was raped, and am the instrument of suffering. One person is hurt and everyone hurts. This is easy to see because we are a community. But it applies to the whole world. In our community there is a sick member. That is all that he is.

"I pray that the rapist gets caught and this never happens again, but if you awake in the night to a rapist in your house, pray immediately to the Virgin Mary, known as Guadalupe in these parts, and ask her to help him and to help you. It may drive him out, this time, before he even rapes you. And speak only Spanish. He wants to hear English."

A pigeon alighting on a statue's sword tip; a child holding his mother's hand, feet flying off the ground running to keep up; a hummingbird at my window; the Great Dane across the road sniffing tires with his best friend the Chihuahua make me weep with a raw tenderness.

Before the rape, I saw egret shit splattered all over park benches. After the rape, I see egret flocks, little puffs of cotton cloud on tree branches.

The article is published eight days after the rape, accompanied by the *Hail Mary* in English and Spanish. In shops all over town, notices appear, in Spanish and English: "Our Sister Beverly was raped. She prayed the *Ave Maria*, and we should, too."

No one knows if the rapist has attacked American women exclusively. A Mexican woman would be much less likely to report a rape; it would ruin her reputation and call shame on her family. And—with good reason—they have no faith that the man will ever be caught or punished.

Now, women all over town clip the prayer from the paper. They keep it by their beds, they carry it in their bags, they memorize it, they pray it.

People begin to say, The energy feels different now. People say, He's going to get caught.

The ex–FBI agent had told me that it takes on average four years to catch a serial rapist. Eight months after he began his attacks, thirteen days after he raped me, five days after the article appeared and people began praying, at 11:00 p.m., on the corner of my street, carrying another rope ladder with hooks attached, the rapist is caught.

> If someone does evil to you,
> you should do good to him,
> so that by your good work
> you may destroy his malice.

> Abbot Pastor, Desert Father

Juan, the special investigator, calls to tell me, "We got the right man. His penis is a peanut. He vomited. Now he's crying in his cell, singing the 'Guadalupana' song."

First response: He got that from me.

Second response: Let him suffer.

Third response: Poor guy. He probably couldn't help himself.

I send the rapist the rosary beads I've prayed on for the past seven years. I got them in Medjugorje; they glow in the dark and were on my altar by my bed, next to the knife. I say, "Tell him to pray. Tell him to ask God for help."

Then because every one of my therapists would say, Feel your anger, I imagine bashing in his head with a cast-iron frying pan.

I cry for the first time. I cry for weeks. I cry for years.

> We can believe that the darkest darkness
> may indeed be a light so bright
> it is blinding our weak eyes.
>
> Jonathan Wilson

I am suspending my disbelief.

I am a snarling dog wagging my tail.

I am cursing God but not admitting it.

All over town people say, He chose the wrong woman to mess with.

I go to a big party with mariachis and bartenders. I dress all in white, like a bride, like a virgin.

People say, Thank you. They say I was so brave.

I am glad that the pen was mightier than the penis.

I am woe is me. I never go to a party, not even a small one for dinner, again.

I can't wait to leave and be anonymous. I can't wait for silence, stillness, a monastery, to heal. I have found the places I want to visit; I make reservations, book my flights. In only three months, I'll go off for half a year, visiting five places. Not all are official monasteries. But I will be silent in every one. I will meditate three times a day, be still as sleep, listen. I will read St. Teresa of Avila, St. Thérèse of Lisieux, St. John of the Cross, Thomas Merton, Bede Griffiths, whom I haven't even heard of yet. I will read interpretations of most of the above. Brother Lawrence will jump off a bookshelf at me; this seventeenth-century monastery cook will be my hero. Joan Chittister, too, Kathleen Norris, Evelyn Underhill, *The Cloud of Unknowing*, *The Imitation of*

Christ, Interior Castle, Abandonment to Divine Providence, Story of a Soul, Sign of Jonah, Son of Man. The Bible. I will feel like I did at seventeen, pushing my baby to the library, taking out Dickens and Austen, Wolfe, Dostoyevsky, Hemingway, Fitzgerald, Faulkner, George Eliot. Book after book after book, like they would save me. Which they did.

I am the rapist's fifth victim. Soon after one of his other victims, Diane (not her real name), was raped, I had dinner with Stewart (not his real name), a guy who lived in an ashram in India and has had visions of saints and encounters with dead people. Stewart and Diane were friends. "I think there's something she needed to learn," Stewart said of what happened to her.

"So, you think bad things happen to people to teach them something?"

"Yes."

"And the Holocaust?"

"That's what everyone brings up . . . Maybe."

"And you think you know what Diane had to learn?"

He hesitated, then nodded. "Maybe."

I didn't want to gossip, so I didn't ask, What?

After I am raped, I run into Stewart on the street. He pulls me into a bear hug, then looks at me and answers the question I don't speak. "I don't know why it happened to you, Bev. I really don't."

I make an appointment with my latest, greatest ex-therapist, Valerie, and ask, "Why did this happen to me?"

She looks confused, or is it scared?

I rephrase: "What do I have to learn?"

She doesn't hesitate. "Compassion. Compassion for others' fears, for others who aren't as strong as you?"

I can see that. But I think there might be more.

+ + +

I call my friend Estrella. For two years in a row, Estrella and I had walked on a three-day pilgrimage to a miraculous Virgin in San Juan de los Lagos, and we'd become friends. Estrella lives in the Ozarks and is a Cherokee. She's also a hermit nun in an order of one, and close to being a holy woman. She calls her two hundred acres the Holy Land. She makes oils, balms, creams, and tinctures from plants she grows and wild plants she finds in the woods. She has a teepee chapel, drums, and a powerful talking stick. Her phone rings all day long with people asking for prayers. Not that long ago she might have been burned at the stake. She once told me that she and God, whom she refers to as the Great Mother, make love every day. I interpret this literally. (Her Holy Land is the third place I'll visit on my monastery tour.)

When I tell her I've been raped, Estrella doesn't seem upset. But she does give me advice: "Pray, 'Open the path and I'll walk it.' "

"God loves to give," she says. "Remember: 'Knock and the door will be opened, ask and you shall receive, seek and you will find.' "

Possible

My friend Geri calls. "Come up *now*. It's an *island*. You couldn't be any safer." I agree. So after the rapist is caught, I arrive ten days early for her wedding on Lake Huron, on a tiny island she and her husband-to-be own with another couple. I pack a wedding outfit, a bathing suit, shorts, mosquito repellent, an icon of Mary I painted for a wedding present.

I hadn't realized it would be a regular social gathering on the island. Geri is fifty, Stephen sixty, best friends who've lived together for nearly thirty years. Stephen, the cook and organizer, comes and goes to the mainland, making wedding-feast preparations. His best friend camps down by the water in a tent. Geri's older brother and his wife are staying in the guest room at the main house. I have my own little bedroom cottage in the woods. There's no lock on my door. This is not what scares me. It's the evil that can come in dreams, in spirit, in the night, through fear. I pray, Please, God, keep evil far away.

I'm convinced my own fear will invite it.

Each morning on my way to the house for coffee, I wave my hands in front of my face, destroying spiderwebs woven across the path from tree to tree overnight, every night. I think I look like a crazy woman waving away bad memories.

+ + +

Everybody knows. But nobody mentions the rape. I feel like when I was twelve and my mother finally bought me a bra; the whole family noticed, but nobody said a word.

Being on an island with five people who know I've been raped feels like my family ritual—the gauntlet: running nude to your room after a bath as everyone rubs their pointer fingers like two sticks making a fire, Shame shame, shame shame.

In Lake Huron, I make myself swim nude in front of anyone.

Then finally, sitting next to Geri out on the deck one night, I cry as I confess it feels verboten to mention the rape.

"Talk all you want," she says. "We didn't know you'd want to."

And so I bring it up, with everyone I meet—for two years. Something like a quarter of all women in the world will be raped at least once. It felt right to do my part in destigmatizing the experience.

Stigmata sounds like shmatta but it's notta. Stigmata are the wounds of Christ. Stigmatists carry the wounds of Christ on their bodies: holes in the palms and feet; a wound in the side, under the heart; punctures around the head from the crown of thorns. The pain is sometimes accompanied by religious ecstasy. Stigmata are also the places on flowers that receive pollen grains. These fertilize the eggs that make the seeds that grow new flowers.

Playing Scrabble and sipping wine on the screened-in porch at sunset, the lake lapping on the rocks below, a guest tells us her stepmother once accused her of not cleaning the kitchen well enough, then rubbed her face raw with a Brillo pad.

"I don't know why I told you that," she says. "I don't like to think about it. I never think about it. It only brings it all back."

I think it's because I told her about my rape and she's kindly sharing to show solidarity.

The rapist should be ashamed, not me.
I refuse to feel shame.
I feel shame, I am shamed.
We hide in the dark what shames us.
Who said, Let there be light? Oh, yeah, God.

Who said that telling your secrets to someone, anyone—bringing them into the light—heals? Freud? It was the original idea behind the sacrament of confession, not punishment, but purging, cleansing, lightening the load, healing.

The first woman who'd been raped in San Miguel is a yoga teacher and a Buddhist. After she gave her statement to the police she made herself difficult to find. And then she refused to testify at the trial. She did not want to dwell on the rape. She wanted to leave the whole incident behind. To testify was to give energy, power, to something that should be allowed to dry up and blow away like a dead leaf. To help deal out punishment would be like throwing fuel on the fire of her own pain. She did not believe in an eye for an eye.

Those were not her exact words. I got them secondhand, and I don't know if Buddhist philosophy would support her in this.

I do not believe in an eye for an eye, either.

This I knew: I did not want that man allowed back on the street to rape another woman. Not to testify seemed no different from being a sociopath.

I judge the Buddhist, and I'm spitting mad at her.

A monk must be like a man who, sitting under a tree,
looks up and perceives all kinds of snakes and
wild beasts running at him.
Since he cannot fight them all,
he climbs a tree and gets away from them.

The monk at all times should do the same.
When evil thoughts are aroused by the enemy,
he should fly, by prayer, to the Lord,
and he will be saved.

Abbot John, a Desert Father

I will fly by jets and prop planes to monasteries, where I will fly by prayer to the Lord. There I will change, be more like Christ— forgiving.

Can you forgive and be judgmental at the same time?

In Mexico, the shaman who'd come to cleanse my house had told me, years earlier when I'd visited him, that I must stop living in, thinking, and writing about my past. It's gone. Be here now, he said. But here and now is the last place I want to be. I want this time to be the past. I want to be in the future, thinking and writing about all this.

This I know: If you deny, disown, ignore the pain, it will come back to bite you—snarly and mean and totally irrational like a rabid dog, or me, every month when I was younger and still PMS-ing.

At night in my little sleeping cottage on Lake Huron I light a candle and stare at the ceiling, thinking, *Now is the time,* no more PMS, hardly any hot flashes, no more mood-altering hormones, a mountain of pain already processed, old now and willing, *now is the time*, raw from a rape, open like a wound, I'm running to the Divine Therapist, I'm laying my self on the line, my arms stretched on a cross, I'm praying, *I surrender. Come to me, please, I hurt, I need, I'm in need. Help! I need You.*

Jesus' beginning point is not sin, it's suffering.

Thomas Merton

One of my best friends, Jacki, arrives with her husband, Will, for the wedding weekend. Jacki and I have been friends for nearly twenty-five years. Years ago, before Jacki met Will, she had an operation on her rotator cuff and couldn't move her arm. She stayed with me and my then-housemate, Renee, in LA, to recover. She asked me to set her hair, and I barked, "Are you kidding? Who's going to see you?" Later, when Renee came home from work, Renee showed me what true kindness was and set Jacki's hair. I don't think Jacki held it against me. She is not thin-skinned, for one thing, and she knows me too well for another.

On Lake Huron, Jacki suggests she and Will and I take a canoe ride. Jacki grew up on a lake in Wisconsin, so she steers in back; Will is a city boy but he's strong, so he paddles in front, while I sit like a queen in the middle as we sluice through the shimmering water, under an enormous blue sky, ducks honk and dive, the air is crystal, the islands we pass a lush vernal green.

"So, Bev," Will says. "How're you doing?"

"I'm okay. Great. Really."

"Is that why you came here early?" Jacki asks me, "to get out of your house, out of that town?"

"No," I protest, offended. Is she accusing me of running away? Of being a coward? I tell Jacki: "Geri invited me. I jumped at the opportunity to be here longer."

"Aren't you afraid to be in your house?" she persists.

"The creep's behind bars. I'll be damned if I'll let that little coward determine my life."

"But aren't you going to monasteries now?"

"I made that decision *before*. It has nothing to do with the rape."

I think but do not say, The rape will change nothing. Absolutely nothing. I may end up in a monastery. I may become a nun. But this will have nothing to do with that rape. I was on my way anyway, I was hunting for monasteries, and the violence interrupted the search, but only for a week or two. I've booked my flights, I've chosen my destinations. I want no one to believe that my choice to join a religious community somewhere, if it happens, has anything at all to do with being a victim, and everything to do with God. It will be a choice made from a position of health and strength, and have nothing to do with fear.

I despise fear.

I decide then and there in that canoe, I will write an article for *O* magazine telling the truth. After all, for a writer, a rape is *material*. I announce this to Jacki and Will. I will begin it with how I'd been looking on the Internet that night for monasteries. The juxtaposition, the irony, will be poignant. Plus, writing about the rape will provide a payday. Remuneration for rape, not a bad thing. I need money for all those suggested donations at the monasteries and retreat centers, for the planes I'll be flying to all those podunk airports.

I tell Jacki and Will how for six months I'll live in nature, woods, desert; twice I'll be eight thousand feet high, and I'll hardly ever speak. I remind them about Soledad, the Benedictine monastery a half-hour from my home in Mexico, how I'd go for a week or weekend and never utter a word while I was there. I remind them about painting icons in San Miguel with a prayer group. How we met every week for years, virtually never spoke besides our opening and closing prayers, and I felt like I knew each of the other women as intimately as my friends, simply by sitting in silence together, praying. As we painted we asked God to guide our hands and we asked help from the saint we were painting, too, usually Jesus or Mary; Jesus being a God and Mary being a saint if you listen to the Catholic Church. I do not tell Will and Jacki that to me God and Mary are the same spirit force energy with different names; Mary was the mother of Christ, but since her death she's become a mystical mother of us all, a feminine manifestation, and in my opinion the feminine side, of a God who is sexless.

Jesus I resist, and have since childhood. His skinny diapered body tortured on a cross, in agony risen up and looking down, could make me feel guilty if it didn't piss me off so much for making me feel guilty. But I'm hoping something will snap, a dart of light will pierce my heart and make me fall miraculously in love with this heroic consciousness-transforming spiritual master. I long to believe He is God made flesh to physically actually walk the earth and show us a *different* way: the way of love. Maybe I will fall in love with Christ, finally, at the monasteries.

I say nothing of this to Jacki and Will. I'm afraid I might have bored them already with so much talk about silence. Unless they're curious or ready, talk of God can shut people down, stop their ears. The sun glints off Jacki's copper hair, kindness is written in Will's soft face. "It's so good to see you," I blurt like a bubble escaping.

"Will was just saying he needed a Bev infusion." Jacki says.

"We've been looking forward to this," Will tells me.

"It's been too long. Let's not go so long again." As soon as I say this I think how I'll be sequestered away and I won't see them for months and months, maybe a year.

We fall silent. Will lays the paddle across his lap, Jacki leans back on her elbows, and we float.

The night before the wedding, on a nearby island in a cottage reserved for wedding guests to which I have moved to make room for more of Geri and Stephen's family, a group of twenty or so takes glasses of wine and gathers in a great room with sofas, stuffed chairs, a fireplace. Someone suggests a game. We are each to tell a story about ourselves, preferably a confession. We can choose to make the story up or tell a true one. After we tell the story, everyone will vote on whether it was true or not. Whoever fools the most people wins. My turn is last. I say, "In high school, right after I got my driver's license, I chased a pigeon around a parking lot until I ran it over. It's haunted me my whole life."

All but one votes that I told the truth, and I win the game. When I told the story, I was near tears. Even though the story had been about my best friend and not me. While I was telling the story it had felt like I'd actually done this.

Later that night, on the eve of Geri and Stephen's wedding, I bunk with Jacki, Will, and Maryann—a newer friend, a corporate lawyer who will wear her tutu tomorrow to officiate at the ceremony. It's like a pajama party. When we finally stop accusing Will of farting, I lie in the dark, thinking about that poor pigeon. And then I remember the eagle. In Mexico the year before, I'd come home to a bucket hanging from a rope in the middle of the back garden wall, which is crowned by a wrought-iron railing. As I puzzled about the bucket, an eagle rose up from the far side of the wall, its ankle attached to the other end of the rope. It flew away for a few yards, but the bucket slammed against the railing and the eagle dropped out of sight, probably dangling by its foot. Its body had been thin enough to fit through the railing, but the bucket was too big. God only knew how long the eagle had been trapped there.

I ran into the street to get help and found Steve, who was building his house two doors away. He retrieved a ladder from his site, and as I held it, he climbed up and cut the rope. The eagle flew under a thorny bush, twenty yards away on the hillside. I worried that the rope would snag on something and the bird would starve or die of thirst. I also thought how, with the grace of God, the bird could peck that twine right off. Later that day, the twenty-one-year-old son of my next-door neighbor came knocking on my door, looking for his bird. The eagle had belonged to him. He'd kept it on their roof, tethered to the bucket that held the water it had needed to live. The bird held captive by the weight of that which sustained it.

The young man had said, "I paid a lot of money for that eagle," implying I'd be responsible for his loss.

To which I snapped, "Get a dog."

As I listen to my roommates breathe deeply and the ruffling of a slight snore, I wonder if I'm captive to some belief I think I'll die without. And then in what seems like a non sequitur, I remember how I hadn't bothered to tell the group that the incident with the pigeon in the parking lot had actually happened; that my best friend had been driving and I'd been in the car. Now I try to remember and can't: Did I shout at Fay to stop, put on the brakes, don't do it? Or did I laugh, cheering her on? I'm capable of both.

I want to be different, to peel off masks, my make-believes, lipstick, to stop making things bigger, more and better, telling white lies improving on, giving an impression.

I will be what you see is what you get.

I will stop hiding cracks and breaks, scars and wounds—from myself, too.

I will be real.

This will take more courage than praying at a rapist did.

I think about Job, how he suffered, lost his family, his friends, his fortune, and ended up a bag of bones covered with smelly oozing boils, how God reduced him to rubble even though Job had been an innocent, kind, abundantly generous, God-worshiping man. Did Job feel like God was punishing him? And if Job did feel this, what did he imagine God was punishing him for? There was so much in my life worth punishing me for—by sending a rapist—if God were vengeful.

God is not tit-for-tat, God is not eye-for-an-eye. And God does not punish. I don't know how, but I know this. I *know* it.

I will have to read the Book of Job again. I will read the entire Old and New Testaments, again. Every word. And I will be enlightened. Later, at, or after the monasteries.

Christ's first public miracle was to offer 150 gallons of delicious, intoxicating wine.

Geri and Stephen stand on a rock. The blue water rocking around them, the fragrant air puffing little breezes like kisses, it is a day more glorious than any in the entire year. They hold each other close, they smile to beat the band, they lock lips strong, Geri throws her hat into the air, and they laugh. They are married.

This time I do not wonder what it would be like to be the bride in a marriage that was not "shotgun" as mine had been—a woman so loved, the Beloved. I don't wonder what I've been missing. I do not boo-hoo about being the last one standing in a game of musical chairs. I suspect I've wasted my life chasing after the wrong thing. Addicted to dreaming the impossible dream, longing only for the exaggerated moments, finding heat in hurt, choosing impossible men. I haven't a clue how to be intimate, and if I ever did have a clue, I lost it a long time ago. Not for the first time I wonder if I will ever consider myself Christ's bride, Christ's beloved. This is what nuns do. I wonder if all the love and energy and devotion I might have given to a husband or lover would be transformed into a different sort of love that is sometimes called Christ love—flowing from me to the whole world, everyone I encounter, and those I don't encounter, too.

It seems possible.

THE MYSTICAL
MONASTERY TOUR

Hush

St. Benedict's Trappist Monastery, Snowmass, Colorado

This is how my six-month, holy-walk-to-God pilgrimage begins: On the plane's descent I look out the window and instead of ribbons of golden aspens winding around the mountains I see ribbons of gray. It's only October 8 and, I'll learn, too late for the aspens to still be gold. But at the time, I interpret their grayness this way: it's turned so cold so fast the poor trees dropped all their leaves while they were still green—no chance for a last hoorah of golden glory. I am not aware of making a connection between their perceived premature deep freeze and my rape. I simply feel indignant—bordering on rage.

I land and drag my ten-ton piece of luggage from the conveyer belt. I'll be staying at St. Benedict's for only eight days but have packed enough for six months and two seasons. I'll begin this trip here in the Rockies and end in springtime Oklahoma.

Since there is no monk in Trappist robes, or anybody else holding a sign with my name on it, I wheel the suitcase along with my carry-on and backpack to a bench, and I sit. And I sit. I'd been told a monk would be here to drive me to the monastery. But first we'll go to a supermarket, where I can buy enough food for my eight-day stay. My own cabin and my own food are reasons I chose St. Benedict's. But there are others: its setting is reputed to be magnificent, and it is home to Thomas Keating, a renowned teacher, writer, and advocate of contemplative prayer, a Christian form of meditation I practice—and plan to practice three times a day. In this centering prayer method, you choose a sacred word, a mantra, which you use when your mind goes off gallivanting to bring you back to center—your deeper self, the still, peaceful place where God is, sometimes called the in-dwelling. A few months before the rape, I had begun using *come* for my sacred word.

I was thinking Jesus might show up.

I'd promised myself that on this pilgrimage, I'd *talk* to Jesus, whom I've resisted since nuns turned me against him when I was a kid. I hope that this time I'll open my heart, reveal my secret self, whisper my hopes, fears, and shame—every day. In fact, I could begin right here on this airport bench, waiting for the monk to show. But instead, because I'm Italian and food-obsessed, I make a mental list of groceries I'll buy. When a half hour passes and there's still no monk, I fight the urge to think but still do think: I'm not welcomed, nothing's working, must be a sign, I never should have come, and why the hell did I choose a male monastery anyway? Short of a papal edict, even if I were Mother Teresa, they couldn't invite me to join.

An hour passes before I finally think to call the monastery. I'm informed that the monk Micah has been here all along, but waiting at the wrong door.

I do not wonder why it took me a godforsaken hour to call.

I do not make an analogy about doors being knocked at, not opened, not found, wrong.

Micah looks as unhappy as I feel. He is not wearing a Trappist monk outfit, but cowboy boots and one of those jackets that looks like it's made from a horse blanket. I'd been looking forward to the white alb with the black scapular—the long bib, front and back—the thick black belt slung low, and I'm trying not to mind that the first monk on my monastery tour resembles a rancher. I resist the urge to blurt, "So, how come you're not in your outfit?"

We are quiet in the car.

I could make conversation, but I'm trying to be genuine. Quiet if I want to be.

At the supermarket I grab a cart and shop while Micah stands by the doors, waiting. I'd read that Trappists are vegetarians. So I buy salami. I never eat salami. And then, naturally, I have to show Micah what I bought. "Looks delicious," he says, smiling.

I feel foolish.

It's nearly eight in the evening when we drive onto the monastery grounds. My hermitage is octagonal and one of eight hermitages on the top of a hill. Micah carries my bag to the door, flicks on the light switch, and points out the thermostat. The place is freezing. I push it up to 68 and bid Micah good evening before shutting the door and turning to my home for the next eight days. It looks brand-new and institutional. Luckily I have no roommate, even though the hermitage accommodates two people. There are two single beds against opposite walls, two desks, two easy chairs, and one round table outside the door of the kitchenette. I put my groceries away and sit.

It's silent as secrets.

I'm alone as a kid in the night calling for a parent who doesn't answer.

I hear a creak on the roof and think I should lock the door.

I am *not* a woman who locks doors at a monastery in the middle of nowhere.

So I don't.

Before I left San Miguel, the ex–FBI agent came by to suggest methods for "securing" my house: bars everywhere, motion detectors, spotlights, razor wire, guard dog.

I do not want to live in a prison that fear built. To lock doors, to never walk alone after dark is to give fear power. I'm not talking about the fight-or-flight instinct: There is danger, and there are predators we should run from. I'm talking about expecting harm and looking for it, then arming yourself—on the chance . . . like those weapons of mass destruction that never existed and started a war.

> Do not be afraid.
>
> The most often repeated phrase
> in the Bible

I hadn't noticed any stars on the ride coming into the monastery, and now I wonder if it's because I never looked up. I shut all the lights and gaze out the window. The sky is overcast and looks as if it's about to snow. I turn on the porch light and watch the tiny flakes drifting down like a dream you can't remember.

After I've unpacked and am snuggled into the narrow single bed, I feel the same excitement I did as a kid sleeping in a tent pitched in the backyard, privileged to be on an adventure, grateful to escape my every day. In the tent I'd felt protected and scared at once, sheltered but outside in the unpredictable dark where a man with a hook for a hand could be lurking. This time nothing about being scared feels like fun.

I cannot give the rapist the satisfaction of having changed me into a woman who locks doors when she is perfectly safe, so I wake up all night long at the slightest creak of the roof, rattle at the window, groan in the settling floor—and I wake at dawn anything but refreshed.

I have made a Rule of Life to follow on my pilgrimage, although I don't yet know that's what it's called. I will meditate three times each day—morning, noon, and early evening—read spiritual books, try to train my mind not to wander and to stay focused on God. I will integrate exercise—yoga and/or walks—into my days; I will eat well, and I will not allow myself to sleep too much.

The first morning, I meditate for forty minutes, then debate whether or not to make breakfast before I leave for Lauds. Time is short, so I decide breakfast can wait, as can yoga. I bundle up, wrap a scarf around my face, and walk out the door.

I have never been in the Rocky Mountains before, and as I walk down the long hill toward the red monastery building nestled in a stand of pines, gaping at the majestic white peaks up in the sky, I think of all those holy mythical mountains, Zion, Horab, Tabor, Fuji. There's a reason that heaven is always pictured as being above. We say, "Things will look up." We say, "Lift your heart. Raise your spirits." We think of "soaring to the heights." And here I am, in the literal heights, God's country, the wild, where bears duck into their winter dens, mountain lions sharpen their claws, herds of elk trundle down paths to the plains. And here I am. I'm a lucky person, I think. But then I remember what I can't wait one day to forget: I was raped.

Followed by, I will never forget being raped.

But I do have my "Rule" to follow. And right now, I am on my way to Lauds. Right now, I remember to keep God in focus, and I pray a rosary until I enter the chapel.

I sit at the back on a raised platform where a few other

retreatants and townspeople also sit, and watch as the fourteen monks walk in and take their seats below, in the center of the chapel amid a dozen or so retreatants and townspeople. The bell rings. We stand, cross ourselves, and sing the Invitatory, "Lord open my lips and my mouth shall declare your praise." At Vespers in late afternoon we will begin with "Oh Lord come to my assistance, my God make haste to help me." I already know this prayer will become a favorite. A cry for help, like dialing 911; you know someone will answer.

After the services, I chant the prayer all the way back up the hill to my hermitage. I make myself a poached egg, read some Merton, do an hour of yoga, and then it's noon and time to meditate again.

This becomes my routine, followed after lunch by a walk down the long dirt road through the monastery grounds, passing pastures with horses in them and large, idle, spidery irrigation machines. Or up a path into the mountains. As I walk I recite the Jesus prayer, like the anonymous Russian monk who'd walked nobody knows for how many years or how many miles reciting, "Lord Jesus Christ, Son of God, have mercy on me, a sinner," until it became the beat of his heart, the electrical current pulsing through his veins.

Usually, by the time I return to the hermitage the light is beginning to fade, and sometimes I nap. I make an early dinner, meditate a third time, read some, and then head off in the dark for vespers.

I had wondered if I'd be able to fill my days, but this is not a problem.

I pray every second I can think to, but I still don't talk, let alone have a heart-to-heart talk with Jesus.

+ + +

In the chapel, everything is clean and simple and beautiful. Unlike a typical cavernous, echoey Catholic church, this is small and intimate, always open, constantly used, a home to these monks in medieval cream-colored robes, who chant the psalms and sit here in silent meditation.

I read in the guestbook in my little hermitage that during community prayer, also called the praying of the hours, we are not to harmonize, sing loudly, or in any way try to be heard above others, that Gregorian chant is meant to be many voices sounding as one.

This is my first intimation of union, except from books, and I receive like a grape on my tongue this instruction to blend in—even as I sit on the raised platform in the back of the chapel and not on the ground floor with the monks like most of the other retreatants and townspeople do. I want in no way to distinguish myself, stick out, be noticed, get attention, talk to anyone. I want to be here but disappeared.

I suspect I might be like an injured animal who's gone off to be alone, to hide and lick my wounds; or I might be like a person in the federal witness protection program, putting on a new identity, but behind the new mask: the same old me.

This is how Merton describes the life of a monk in *The Sign of Jonas*: "The whole day is supposed eventually to become a prolonged prayer in which the monk remains united with God through all his occupations."

If attention is love, and I believe that it is, just imagine giving God all your attention. Imagine dedicating every little lowly activity to God.

Imagine God giving you attention back.

Imagine God watching you wash a floor.

I was engaged once to a schoolteacher while attending community college as a young mother with a first-grader. I'd come home from classes to find that he'd washed my floors and was cooking dinner. It had made me feel more loved than any declaration, flower bouquet, or caresses ever had. When a different lover, with whom I'd lived, knelt beside the bathtub and bathed every inch of my body, I'd felt both like a baby cared for unconditionally and a woman cherished.

Maybe attention from God will feel like this.

I never told either man how their loving attention had made me feel. I don't remember even saying thank you. I was the one to break it off with each of them. Intimacy and I are like détente between two nations engaged in a cold war.

Every day, I think I will talk to Jesus.

I've read about a practice called Imaginative Prayer, also called the Ignatian method of *Lectio Divina*, and I have planned to try it. You imagine a biblical scene, smell the smells, hear the sounds, feel the air, then insert yourself. I think of the scene with the Samaritan woman, a disreputable woman, considered unclean, whom Jesus talks to all alone, I think, a bit flirtatiously. He lets her know that he knows her, that he sees who she really is.

It's a sexy scene.

And I can't do it. I can't imagine the scene and I can't talk to Jesus in real time or in imagined biblical time. I don't even try.

Fear can hold us back
for faith is a journey into the unknown.

Basil Hume

As soon as I graduated college, at twenty-seven, I moved
to New York, where I'd always wanted to be, and lived in an apartment with my son and a couple hundred cockroaches. Those days
my drink of choice was Stoli on the rocks, and after a few of those
I became who I thought of as the Real Me: sassy, punky, bad-ass,
and cool. Flirting and playing pool one night with a gorgeous
young lawyer with hair the color and wave of a cocker spaniel's, I
was so confident, lit, wise-cracking, and in-my-body saunter that
I even won the pool game. We made love on his king-sized bed,
our clothes strewn on the shiny hardwood floors, with not a cock-
roach in sight. We slept cuddled beneath a white downy comforter, our heads on pillows soft as clouds. I don't normally like
aftershave, but the scent of it on him produced visions of summers in the Hamptons, New Year's Eve in Paris.

In the morning I had to fly. I probably believed this impulse
to fly a desire to be free. I now know I didn't want him to see me
in the light of day, when I'd turn into a pumpkin, the real Real
Me, whose teenage son was back home in their tenement waking
up alone, a would-be, unpublished, writer who never wrote—
with exactly ten bucks to her name. I fished in my jeans pocket.
Make that not a penny to her name, because, as happened so often, I'd left every red cent of change on the bar.

Before I could make my escape, the young lawyer sat up.
"Hey," he said. "It's Saturday. Where're you going?"

I would have loved to go get breakfast, a Bloody Mary, stroll
over to Washington Square, browse in used bookstores, take in a

movie, hold hands, tell stories, kiss. I could always call my son, Jason, let him know I'd be gone the whole day. It wouldn't be the first time.

"Yeah?" I said, no doubt looking like a dog trying not to lick her chops because she'd been beaten every time she went for the offered bone. I could think of not one more word to say, I had no flirty follow-through; I had a tied tongue.

Without his eyes moving from mine, he looked me up and down. "You're different today."

I was out of there so fast I must have appeared a blur.

Psychologists and theologians talk about the false self, the masks you wear, the person you make yourself into to ward off pain. Your self-image is another way to refer to it, your ego, or your "act."

Your true self is the seed of the soul that was in you when you were born, it is you in the original, before the rewritings, embellishments, the walls of denial, your fortresses erected to protect you from pain. It is who God made you to be; it is the divine inside of you. It is what Christ saw when he looked at the Samaritan woman at the well.

It's painful when who you want to be and who you really are collide.

Only by looking at the pain, by feeling it, giving it attention, loving it, does it release, or is it transformed.

I awake too late to meditate this morning, and after I eat a rice cake smeared with almond butter I rush to Lauds. This day, I do not sit at the back of the chapel but down on the main floor, where the monks sit in two rows. I sit behind them on a bench along the wall. At the far end of this chapel is a plain wooden table: the altar. In back of and above the altar is a tall, slim stained-glass window, where a young doe-eyed Mary looks out at you, holding her baby, Jesus.

I've read the Gospels many times and have admired Jesus, how he went apoplectic when faced with hypocrisy. "You hypocrites!" he called the priests of his day. He refused to obey the letter of the law, insisting instead on looking at an issue with your heart. Jesus, a lowly peace-loving peasant, a rod of truth his only weapon, healed the lame, the wounded, the possessed, lepers, the hemorrhaging, the deaf, the blind; he raised the dead.

Jesus was a free-thinking radical, revolutionary hero. I could admire him from a distance, like Gandhi or Martin Luther King. But loving Jesus was a stretch, like loving some exotic food you've only heard described.

He has put in my heart a marvelous love.

Psalm 16

Two months after the rape, I babysat my one-year-old grandson, Zachary, for ten days. I took him on a road trip to visit friends, and he ran me ragged. Every time Zach and I sat down to eat, he climbed down from his chair and took off. I didn't know whether to make him stay seated and eat or not. I handed him a whole tomato like an apple, which he ate dripping all over himself, running outdoors with my friend's three dogs. I took him to the beach and let him play nude in the sand. I didn't know if this was acceptable, because sand would probably get up his bum. I didn't know any more about caring for a one-year-old now than I had at eighteen; I didn't know if my development had been stunted or if everyone struggles with these questions when they're caring for a kid. That night when I bathed Zach and lifted him out of the water, sand lined the tub like incriminating evidence. He had dark circles under his eyes. My heart felt like two hands had reached in to twist it. In his jammies he sat on my lap for a story, his hair damp under my chin, smelling clean. His dimpled hands rested on mine as I turned the pages, and I felt so much love, it overflowed in tears. "I love you, Zachy," I whispered, kissing the top of his head. Yes, he nodded.

After I put him down in his porta-crib at the foot of my bed, I went to bed, too. Zach fell right to sleep, and, listening to the rhythm of his breath, I got scared and thought, What if Zach grows up to be a junkie. That's what my ex-husband—his grand-father, now dead—grew up to be.

At that apocalyptic thought I remembered to ask God to pro-tect Zach. And to please sustain me through this love, to help me not only give more than enough love, but to endure it—and not be so afraid.

This I have heard:
　Love has the highest energy vibration and fear the lowest.
　Sin is anything that takes you away from God.
　God is love.
　Sin is anything that takes you away from loving.

This I have also heard:
　We are not punished *for* our sins, we're punished *by* them.

Near the end of my stay at St. Benedict's, I walk down the dirt road to Lauds and mass, praying the Jesus prayer, when a mem-ory arrives, from the morning I ran from that young lawyer. It had been early, maybe seven a.m., and as I hurried home, a deliv-eryman with an enormous bouquet crossed my path. He bowed and said, "If these flowers belonged to me, lady, I'd throw them at your feet. You just made my day."

+ + +

That was how the Samaritan woman felt when she encountered Jesus.

All those years ago, if I'd let him, the deliveryman could have cooled—at least a little—the scorch I was feeling. All those years ago, if I'd believed in God, I could have viewed the deliveryman as a messenger.

In chapel with the monks, the bell rings. We stand, bow, then pray, "Oh God, come to my assistance, my Lord, make haste to help me," and I feel my heart take a deep breath as the chapel seems to whisper, "Hush now," like a mother when, for the moment, her child's finished all her crying.

At My Shoulder

I will lead you into the desert
and there I will speak to your heart.

Hosea

Years before I was raped, years before the monastery tour, I was signing copies of my book *Riding in Cars with Boys* with Drew Barrymore at a store in Los Angeles. Two young men I had not seen in a few years—TV writers and friends, with whom I'd briefly written on a sitcom—stood in front of us and handed me a book to sign. They were team comedy writers my son's age and had once had a crush on me. I was delighted to see them, and not only because they were probably the only people on that mile-long line who'd come to see me and not Drew. And then one of them said, grinning, "We hear you're a Born Again." The implication being: They had to come see this for themselves.

"What?" I was horrified that this is what people were saying about me. At that point, my book about the Virgin Mary had come out, and I would have liked a relationship with her son—or so I believed—but it hadn't happened yet.

Still, I'd read the gospels enough to know it was not cool to deny Jesus. Which is what I proceeded, more or less, to do. "I'm in love with the Virgin Mary, not Jesus," I said. Mary is easy to claim. She's a *mother*; no religion was named after her; no wars were fought, no one was tortured on a rack, burned at the stake, or otherwise murdered in her name. But because of what we've done in his name, poor peace-loving Jesus is another story.

And then there's the religious right that claims Jesus as its own, the social conservatives, the family values bell ringers, who "value the sanctity of human life" but support the death penalty, and refuse funding to programs that provide food and clothing and medical care to those fetuses once they grow into children who need them.

It's entirely possible that my resistance to having a relationship with Jesus is because I'd then have to admit to it.

Yes. I am that shallow, that worried about what people think of me—and I do believe my soul depends on letting go of this, dropping my "image."

I hope I'm finally, truly, really, honestly, heart-and-soul willing to love Jesus. I just don't know if I'm able.

Before I left Snowmass for my next stay, at Nada Hermitage, in Crestone, Colorado, I read a testimony by a man who wrote of inviting Christ to take the front seat of a bicycle built for two—a graphic version of AA's famous "Let go, let God." I decided to try that out, then endured a snowstorm, two delays, a missed flight, and enough turbulence in a prop plane to make me fear for my life. (This made me realize dying would be a relief—and that I have no idea if this is a sign of depression or faith.) I'd done pretty well all day, looking for meaning in the delays, noticing the silver linings. While trapped in the Denver airport for four hours, I'd been able to play with a little boy my grandson's age, which allowed his mother to go to the can in peace. I made a few overdue, heartening phone calls; and a cashier at a bookstore gave me a 30 percent discount when I told him I'd missed my flight.

But then, eleven hours later, after landing in Alamosa, still an hour from Crestone, tired, hungry, the silver lining threatening thunder, I climbed into the Little Stinkers Cab—so named I reckon because it smelled like ten thousand cigarettes were smoked in it yesterday—I felt like I might puke, and any thoughts of Jesus, God, surrendering, gratefulness, turning potholes into stepping-stones flew right out the cranked-down car window.

I'm so late, it's dark when the cab pulls in front of Nada's main building, an adobe-looking structure called Agape, and I can get little sense of the landscape. I know it's eight thousand feet above sea level and have been told that because it's hermit week, and the five monks—three women and two men—are in solitude and silence, no one would greet me, but a map to my hermitage would be taped to the table. So I'm surprised to find waiting for me a youngish woman (late thirties, I guess) in jeans, who introduces herself as Sister Kay. Sister Kay was worried I wouldn't be able to find my way to the hermitage in the dark, so she's been waiting for me. We walk out, she hands me a flashlight and directs the cabdriver down a narrow dirt road. We drive around the building and then on tire tracks down a slight hill to a hermitage named Gandhi, my tiny new home for the next month.

By tiny, I mean three and a half giant steps long and three wide. I've rented storage units bigger than this. My luggage takes up half the living space. Why had no one warned me how small this hermitage is? I'm even more hungry and tired now, and my heart is fluttery, not in a good way. I really don't want to cry, but the hot plate is a single and the refrigerator's the size of a wall safe. The only place to wash dishes is in the bathroom, and the place gives the overall impression of being shabby, even stingy. I collapse onto the only armchair. It is not comfortable.

I move to the bedroom nook, where a twin bed is wedged

between the walls. In the corner on a tiny shelf, Mary in an icon holds baby Jesus' butt in her hand and looks directly at me, which is unusual in icons. But Mary's expression is common; her eyes seem to be saying that she understands our unfortunate human condition perfectly, and it makes her sad.

I lie down on the bed, which is a platform with a piece of foam—firm the way I like it—and close my eyes. Nada is in the desert, in the tradition of the Desert Fathers and Mothers, who lived in caves and huts. Moses led his people to the desert for a reason. In the desert there is lack. We're most likely to turn to God when we're in need. That's why Christ considered being poor a boon to the spirit. That's why Christ said it's hard for a rich man to enter the kingdom of heaven, and he wasn't talking about the afterlife.

The desert is an outward manifestation of how we feel inside: thirsty for something more. When I was in college and still idealistic, I used to say I never wanted to be comfortable, that too much comfort makes you fat and slow. Discomfort sharpens your senses, and deprivation, what you don't have, makes you grateful for what you *do*.

I open my eyes and notice the ceiling is constructed of pine planks, tongue and groove. The place smells of pine. The comforter is homemade and has been washed so many times it's soft as a baby's cheek. It smells like soap and the outdoors. When I stand up, it occurs to me to look under the bed. My suitcase will tuck nicely in there.

I notice that on the windowsill above the counter in a small basket someone has placed two golf-ball-sized homegrown tomatoes, a banana, a potato, an onion. Someone has placed cans of food in the cupboard, granola, olive oil, pasta, rice. On the wall is a framed Gandhi quote written in calligraphy, about walking on the edge of a sword. "He who strives never perishes," Gandhi says.

I was raped five months ago and will now live in a little house under the great Western sky, with nothing to do but pray and read and worship—in a place that honors Gandhi and the Virgin Mary.

What's the problem?

I peel the banana and take a bite. I step outside, where the midnight-blue sky is so thick with glittering stars it vibrates. I breathe in the cool desert air. Had I known this line from a psalm, it may have arrived:

> This is the day the Lord made . . .
> Rejoice and be glad.
>
> Psalm 118

I heard about Nada from a Buddhist friend who'd toured the Holy Land and each night for two weeks was lectured to by representatives from different spiritual traditions. He'd been most impressed with the two monks from Nada, and the Nada website was among the first I'd looked at. Nada, a.k.a. the Spiritual Life Institute, is in the Carmelite tradition. The monks wear beige robes with dark brown scapulars and call themselves apostolic hermits. This appears to mean that they value silence and solitude yet run retreat centers in Ireland and Colorado, publish a magazine, occasionally teach and give lectures, and embrace a moderate rhythm of communal prayer, while also praying, and living, alone in their own hermitages. The community is composed of men and women, four members in Ireland and five in Colorado.

"Be still and know that I am God" are words from Psalm 46 on Nada's website. I don't remember which monasteries I bookmarked the night I was raped, but if I did read Isaiah's words then, I'm sure they seemed mysterious and wise. Or I might have interpreted them more prosaically, as an invitation to stop my obsessive searching on the Web, close my laptop, be still, and go to sleep. I do remember noticing that it was past midnight and dark as ink, without a moon. I turned onto my side and went out like a light. It was probably less than an hour later that I was awakened by a wave of movement, a sinking, shifting weight on the mattress, a tug on the sheet. My eyes flew open, my heart abuzz like a hornet's nest, and I knew the last thing I wanted to know: What I'd dreaded all my life was here.

And it still is. This moment of shocking awareness in the dark that there's a rapist in my bed repeats like a refrain.

My first night at Nada I have a nightmare: The rapist hovers over my bed, and I wake myself screaming. For a while, evil remains a presence in the room as real as a gaping door you know you've shut.

I pray the St. Michael prayer. I pray, "Please, dear God, keep evil far away." I pray, "Hail Mary, full of grace . . ." I pray, "Hail Holy Queen . . . our life, our sweetness, and our hope . . ." I pray, "God come to my assistance, my Lord make haste to help me." Eventually, perhaps two hours later, the prayers lull me to sleep.

When I awake again in the night, I pray again.

In the morning light, the terrors are easy to dismiss. Like how you wet your bed when you were a kid—sort of irrelevant now.

In the morning light, my first sight is of a mammoth flat-topped rocky mountain to the east, looming over everything. I'll learn that it's a 14,000-footer called Challenger but the monks call it Mount Carmel, after the mountain in Palestine where in the early thirteenth century their spiritual ancestors had fled their societies to live as a band of hermits. I make coffee and watch through floor-to-ceiling windows as the sun rising behind

Carmel spreads light over an oceanic burnt-gold valley. I'll learn it's called the San Luis Valley, that its area is the same as Rhode Island's, that there have been numerous UFO sightings.

The hermitage is quiet as whispers. I hear my own breath, my bare feet on the floor.

To provide insulation, the north wall of my hermitage is backed into a sand dune. It's passive solar, which means that during the day the cabin is heated by sunlight streaming through floor-to-ceiling windows facing south. Through the windows I see scrubby bushes growing in sand, deer nibbling on them, bunnies nibbling too or hopping by, and a flock of pinyon jays shows up many afternoons, making a racket like a gang of adolescents. Through the windows I look out across the prairie to the southern horizon and to the west the rolling San Juans. Over it all reigns an enormous, sea-to-shining-sea, sunrise-to-sunset sky. I can hardly believe I'm actually where the deer and the antelope play; sometimes I just have to sing "Home on the Range."

Most days the sun is so hot I have to keep the door open, and then bucketfuls of sand blow in. When it's cloudy or snowing, as it is this day toward the end of my first week, I keep the door closed and make a fire, wear a scarf, knit hat, and fleece jacket. The snow falls so thickly I can barely make out my woodpile. Agape, the main building three hundred feet away, has disappeared, as has Carmel beyond it. I'm cozy, in a snow bubble, feeling like a kid on a porch in the rain. I open the music library on my computer, direct it to play songs randomly, and here Joni Mitchell comes singing "Woodstock," stardust and garden.

Whenever I hear Joni Mitchell I think of my women's group back in the early 1970s. Feminists and proud of it, we looked at our own socially conditioned behaviors, beliefs, and misbeliefs, and discussed how we could change them. If we changed ourselves, we believed, we'd change the world. I still believe this. It's hard to imagine, but until a few years before I joined that women's group, practically the only thing the women I knew did alone outside of their own houses was go to the toilet—but not the bathroom. If you were on a double date and had to go, the other woman went with you. So, on principle, one Sunday, after having broken up with my boyfriend, I drove all by myself for a half hour to the Peabody Museum in New Haven. I hardly looked at an exhibit; I watched couples holding hands, families gathered in front of dinosaurs, and felt as conspicuous and lonely as a kid waiting in line at a Ferris wheel while everyone else takes seats two by two.

Now I can think of nothing I'm afraid to do alone besides camping, because I haven't tried it yet. I know women who camp alone all the time, but I don't know a single woman who must be accompanied to the restroom. The world can, and does, change.

Still, I can't help thinking that my younger, sexually active, feminist self would have been horrified to see me sequestered in a shoe-box cabin in a monastery. I'd have to explain to her that even though it's true that I totally enjoy not having to converse with anyone, my solitude isn't about being alone, and I don't feel lonely. A nun in an interview was asked what she did while she was in solitude, and she answered, "Let God love me."

I am anticipating plenty of solitude at Nada. The schedule of communal worship is much less frequent than at Snowmass. Rather than every day, mass is four times a week, vespers twice, and Lauds once. Other than perhaps when I help the monks clean after Lauds on Saturday mornings—which, like everything else here, is voluntary—and Sunday brunches after mass, I'm expecting never to speak.

So I'm a little surprised when at my first Sunday brunch, Kay, the monk who'd met me the night I arrived, suggests she come by for a talk on Monday.

The next morning, I invite Kay in, offer her the armchair, pour her a cup of tea, sit across from her, and smile. "How are you?" she asks, really asking.

"I'm so—" I don't have words. I take a deep breath, shake my head. "Grateful."

Kay's face lights up. "Wonderful."

Then I launch into the story of my rape.

"I'm so sorry." She bends over her knees to lean in closer. "How are you feeling?"

"Fine," I say as my lips start to tremble. "I don't know why I'm getting upset. Well, actually, I awake a lot in the night, terrified." I tell her that in my five nights here, I've had nightmares twice. "Still . . . I'm so happy."

"Maybe you feel safe here. Safe enough to feel the fear. If you ever need help or company, please, don't hesitate."

As she writes down a phone number, I repeat to myself, *safe enough to feel the fear,* then let it go.

"You've been through a trauma," Kay says. "It's natural to feel scared. I know." She seems to imply she's had a similar experience, which I appreciate even if her sharing is done cryptically. "It takes time. I know that's a cliché, but it's true. It does get better . . . I don't know how much you know about the community . . ."

She explains that the founder, their charismatic leader, had to be removed five years before because of sexual misconduct, which apparently had been occurring for years. Almost half of the members had left, and those who've remained are still reeling from the aftershock.

I try to give a little support. "Those charismatic spiritual leaders are the worst."

"The brighter the light, the bigger the shadow, they say." Kay's smile has a measure of wince in it. "How are you doing spiritually?" she asks. "How's your relationship with God?"

She's the first person to ever ask me that question, and I want to hug her. "Good. Good. Great. Evolving," I say, then ask, "Would you answer a question? Do you really think of Jesus as your spouse, literally as your husband?" St. Teresa of Avila, St. John of the Cross, St. Thérèse of Lisieux, whom I've been reading, overflow with romantic images, gush with endearments. "I mean," I restate to Kay, "do you feel *in love*?"

She opens her eyes wide as though jokingly admitting to a secret pleasure. "Yes, we do."

Then she asks if we could talk again during my stay, concerned, I'm sure, about my night terrors.

I am, too. Nighttime is not so quiet here. Because the cabin is backed into a sand dune, the roof is almost level with the ground, and sometimes a deer jumps onto it with a loud thud, startling me awake, sending me into paroxysms of sweaty prayers again; sometimes it sounds like a few animals are having a square dance up there. And that sends me into panic prayer mode, too.

In the daytime, I feel both blissful and as though I'm in spiritual training, learning methods of prayer and new ways of being, arming up with techniques, as though I'm preparing for battle. Only, I'm not sure with whom or what I'm going to war—other than myself. Maybe life.

Most of my learning is found in books. In *Practical Mysticism*, Evelyn Underhill educates me about being a mystic. Forget about stopping to merely *smell* the roses; throw open the windows you don't even know are slammed shut over your eyes, see, experience, smell that rose for its own sake, not your own, see it as a manifestation of divinity—and the pebble under your shoe, too. See with the eyes of love, experience awe, perceive that everything is in union with everything else and all of it is in union with the One.

It won't be easy. It will take simplifying one's life, disciplining

one's mind, many hours in quiet recollection and contempla-
tion. Then one day, perhaps, there will no more "log" in my eye,
no more ego getting in the way, and I will fill with radiance, be
an agent of light, one who helps change the world. (I figure it
could take a few lifetimes, but there's no time like right now to
begin.)

In *Practicing the Presence of God*, Brother Lawrence, a
young foot soldier in seventeenth-century France who became a
Carmelite monk, gives practical advice. Brother Lawrence says
that you don't have to be in chapel to pray to God, because God
is always here every second and loves hanging out with you, all
he requires is a little attention, a thank-you, a word of praise,
even pleas for help. Brother Lawrence was a cook who hated to
cook but loved "flipping [his] little omelet for the love of God."

It's after reading St. Teresa of Avila's three books that I
finally find the courage to get close to Jesus.

Freud would probably call St. Teresa a hysteric. She suffered
from debilitating bouts of illness; had visions and raptures, heard
locutions; would levitate in chapel, while trying vainly to hold herself on the ground and not invite attention. I read *A Life*, her auto-
biography; *Interior Castles*, her book on the seven stages of prayer;
and *The Way*, a sort of spiritual instruction manual for the nuns in
the monasteries she founded; and it's not long after I begin them
that that late starter, hyperbolic digresser of startling magnitude,
that drama queen; reluctant author; courageous reformer; that
gushing fainter in the wings; that visionary doctor of the church;
instructor of mystical prayer; that levitating, body-tortured, self-
negating powerhouse ardent lover of Christ, able to outsmart the
church's male-dominated envy-riddled inquisition-mongering hierarchy; the mother-founder of this monastery's tradition; and my
teacher and unlikely friend leads me by example one night into the
empty chapel.

St. Teresa makes me wonder if my fear of loving Christ, and my resistance to trying, is the dark inside of me arguing down the light. Teresa, like the Desert Fathers and Mothers, refers to the "evil one" all the time. Usually when she does, she's talking about her own thoughts, thoughts that make her yearn for what could be harmful, thoughts that are criticisms, judgments of others, beliefs about her own limitations. At one point, when she writes about feeling ill and depleted so much of the time, she says that once she realized it was the devil who was telling her this, she had more than enough energy for everything she wanted to do, and her body felt fine.

St. Teresa would often be distracted and have to bring a book to chapel while the other nuns meditated. She had a breakthrough in prayer when she imagined herself into the scene in the Garden of Gethsemane, where Christ agonized before the crucifixion. I decide that I'll use that scene, too.

Late one night, I take my flashlight and walk to the triangular-shaped chapel. I read the signs in the vestibule: "Let not my thanks to thee . . . rob my silence of its greater homage," by Tagore; and "Take off your shoes . . . for the place on which you stand is holy ground" (Exodus 3:4–6). I take off my shoes, then enter the chapel and bow.

It's small and intimate, with two sets of rows of upholstered chairs angled toward each other, in perfect view of the altar at a tip of the triangle. Down two steps is the "pit," where during services the monks sit on benches in a pie-shaped area in front of the altar. I switch on only the ceiling light illuminating Jesus, who floats above the altar on his cross, and sit in the pit crosslegged on the floor.

Leaning my back against the seat of a bench, I look up at him the way I do through mass. The crucifix is almost life-size and dominates the intimate space. It's an Ascension crucifix, which means Christ is about to fly up to heaven. Jesus is metal and seems to be straining off the wooden cross, his hair lifting with the wind of rising. During my orientation I'd been told that although Jesus' body appears to be metal, parts of it are wood. His chest and legs, arms, feet, hands—which lift off the cross—are indeed metal, but the middle of his torso, his belly and guts, are wood and sunken in the cross. The wood symbolizes matter, earth, the material world, and the metal, matter transformed into spirit. Jesus is both man and God, divine and human, flesh and spirit. Jesus' expression is astonishingly vivid, caught in the split second between pain and release, agony and ecstasy, despair and joy, here and where he's going. At the same time he looks like he could be named Stanley.

I close my eyes and imagine Jesus in the Garden of Gethsemane. He's on his knees, and has been on them all night. I hear an owl hoot, the snap of a twig as an animal passes by. It's pleasantly cool and would be a beautiful night if Jesus, and I, didn't know what will happen tomorrow.

Jesus is sweating. I can smell perspiration with a stain of fear in it. Jesus is so frightened he sweats drops like blood.

A little ways down the hill, the apostles John and Peter and James, whom Jesus had asked to stay up with him, are sleeping under a tree. Jesus has been telling them what will happen tomorrow, but they haven't had ears to hear. That's why they're sleeping even though Christ has asked them to stay awake with him. They're in denial. They hadn't had the ears to hear so much of his teachings. Like everyone else, they'd expected a messiah of power and glory, a conquering hero. Sure, he'd cured the crippled, the blind, the possessed; he'd raised a few from the dead, but what good was it all if he was going to die tomorrow— defeated, powerless, in full-frontal nudity for everyone to see.

Jesus knows his work hasn't been successful. His good news

changed so little. People flocked to him for miracles, but nobody really wanted to follow his teachings: Love your neighbor as yourself, forgive, forgive, and forgive again, turn the other cheek, if you have two coats give one away, the meek shall inherit the earth, be as little children, the last shall be first. They couldn't even take in the ones that are easy to swallow: "I have come so you can have life and have it to the full; full measure, pressed down, shaken together, running over, and pouring into your lap."

Jesus is sad and tired; he's spent and despairing, and, I think, afraid of what will happen tomorrow.

A lump forms in my throat when I hear, "If it is your will, let this cup pass from me. But not my will. Yours."

I kneel next to him. I do not want to intrude. I won't speak. I want to transmit love; I want him to know that someone is with him. He's not alone. He has a friend.

Teresa felt too sinful, too unworthy, to hold Jesus' hand or wipe his brow.

I feel that way, too.

"I love you," I say, and then I feel it, a chestful of almost lusty feeling, but tender, like holding an infant.

For the first time, I wonder what it would mean to help God.

> Your opening and his entering are but one moment.
>
> Meister Eckhart

At night as I lie in bed terror-struck, it's not exactly the physical act of rape I think of or react to so much as everything that attended it: being under another's control, the binding of my will, the threat of more violence and humiliation, the tang of evil stinking the air like a dead skunk.

I think it all adds up to this: What I'm dreading is my own fear.

I think how in the Garden, Christ knew that all of those horrors I just mentioned were going to happen to him the next day, with the possible exception of evil stinking the air like a dead skunk. But maybe it did.

When Christ was tempted in the desert by Satan, resisting all the wily one's temptations, it says in Luke, "And Satan left— *for a time*." Maybe Satan returned and was in the Garden of Gethsemane.

I'm not sure I even believe in Satan.

But I believe in evil. And I believe fear bows at the feet of evil, and I believe that the dark presence that wakes me and lingers in my room, the presence that causes me so much fear, is evil.

I do not hold on to this, because I'd rather not believe this. It's too scary.

I suspect that like the history teacher in my high school, a World War II vet who'd dive under a desk when he heard a loud noise, thinking it was a bomb, I'm suffering from posttraumatic stress disorder. His trigger was a loud bang, but mine, because it happened when I was sleeping at night, is probably the dark and sleep.

"God," I pray all the time, "heal me."

Again in a dream, the dark hovering figure begins to bend toward me, but this time I'm awakened by three loud knocks. I lie in bed sweating, my heart drumming in my ears, believing there's someone at my door, waiting to hear if he will knock again, if I'll hear him walk away. When I hear nothing more, I wonder if God knocked to save me from the nightmare.

I'm meditating in the armchair, and I experience rather than actually remember a very early time, a time before I came to believe I was not good enough. This was a time when I still knew love, because it had been there when I was born, had accompanied me into this life. Perhaps the time lasted only until the age of two. Back then, the moon and the sun and the stars were inside of me, so were birdsong and the tree so majestically tall in my yard. I loved them all and they loved me, but it wasn't like that. They were in me and I was in them.

It snows large floating flakes. I look out over the valley and see flake behind flake all the way to the horizon as though frozen in a frame; one picture, many snowflakes, all of them falling, distinct and separate, different and the same—together falling. Snow.

I sit in the armchair to meditate, plant my feet a foot apart on the floor, sit up tall, close my eyes, and in what feels like no time, I open my eyes. It's forty minutes later. I did not fall asleep, I was nowhere, I was nothing, nada. Peaceful. Floating.

Without announcement, or consciousness, at a moment I cannot recall, as subtle as waking from sleep, Christ is at my right shoulder. As present as if sitting in a dark room, you sense someone standing a half foot away. Palpable, although ephemeral, as heartening as your best friend and neighbor watching your back, comforting as coming home to the smell of dinner in the oven.

Snow crunches beneath our boots as Kay and I walk on a path by a rushing stream. I tell her I can feel Christ at my shoulder. Right now, and every moment since he first appeared.

"Which shoulder?"

"The right."

She nods as though she knew it all the time.

I tell her about losing time in meditation, the three knocks that woke me from the nightmare. The snow.

Kay says I'm being given spiritual consolations—gifts along the way, graces offered to beginners to keep me on the path. And that, almost certainly, they won't last.

I believe it has to be different for everyone and hope these gifts keep raining down.

Questions I did not ask Kay (probably because I doubt she or anybody has the answers):

Are these nightmares symptoms of posttraumatic stress disorder or are they spiritual consolations, deepening my need for God? Is it possible for them to be both?

Is the hovering figure evil?

And is the devil coming near because I'm drawing close to God?

This is what I understand about what Christians call Christ's passion: After he suffered all the agony, he died and rose from the dead. This is an illustration of how God uses our pain: We suffer deeply and our ego dies—at least for a time. And this is where the opportunity lies, to be born again into a new life, with new eyes—to be transformed.

Christ's passion is an act of self-sacrifice, an act of love—to show us that God suffers, too.

Christ said, Take up your cross and follow me. Is your cross to bear whatever makes you suffer? Is my cross to bear the rape? What does take up your cross, which is the suffering from my rape, mean? To accept it, to feel it?

+ + +

Did the rape deepen a need for God, opening wide a space that might have remained only a crack? And is it through this space that so much light is streaming in?

A statement I didn't make to Kay:
 Since the rape, I am closer to God than I have ever been.
 Since the rape, I am more frightened than I have ever been.

As my time at Nada draws to an end, even though I have new places and adventures ahead, I'm not sure I want to leave. The five community members are all within ten years of my age. They are three nuns, a priest, and a brother, vibrant and athletic. I have eaten with them four times at Sunday brunch and, for one entire day, stuffed and addressed envelopes for a mailing. When we were done, at dusk, Eric, the priest, broke out a few bottles of their homemade wine, someone produced cheese and crackers, and we sat around the kitchen table, a few times melting into giggling fits. They are lighthearted, make me laugh, and I'm impressed that even the women take turns giving Sunday homilies, and how each one interprets the scripture—often in surprising ways—as a lesson in loving.

On the Sunday afternoon before my last day, I sit in the periodical room off the library and hear Connie, one of the nuns, and Eric in the kitchen cooking a meal the community will share that evening in a building reserved for their use, and I feel a pang in my chest: for Sunday dinners with my family, which I have experienced only rarely since all us kids grew up. Dinner with a community—with brothers and sisters—might feel similar, each sibling sometimes annoying and always familiar, no pretenses that go unnoted, and lots of teasing. Only these brothers and sisters wouldn't be related by blood but by the choices we've made that have brought us to this place, by our shared belief in something ephemeral and huge, both beyond and part of ourselves, by our trying to make God the ground of everything.

Communities usually require a probationary period, during which they get to know and observe you, and you them. It's rather like a courtship, and if there's a mutual fit, it's followed by an engagement, called the novitiate. If both parties are still interested after that, you marry, or take vows: a life-long commitment. Depending on the community, the process can take from three to five years. I have been known after only a few dates to jump into living with a man. And never once did I stick it out till marriage. (I was married at seventeen, but that was different. I was pregnant.) I do realize I'm beginning to apply the same logic concerning Nada as I've applied to my relationship with men: I could come and live here; I don't have to commit; I can always leave. But this time, I'm also thinking, God will let me know if this is right. Besides, I have no idea if I could endure the desert dryness, the fierce sun, harsh climate; 20-below-zero winters with the only heat coming from the sun and a woodstove that runs out of wood before the night's half over. I don't know if such routine solitude would feed me or eventually become too lonely to bear; whether, in living in any monastery, I'd be running away from life or immersed in it. And from the community's perspective, what would I have to contribute? Considering my advancing years, they could rightly view me as a liability, about to go arthritic.

When I asked Kay on our walk if they ever accept novices, she told me that the community is in no position to consider a new member—of any stripe. The community is still reeling from the shake-up when the founder left and trying to reimagine itself, a task that the nine members, five in Colorado and four in Ireland, would gather to carry out in the coming year.

I am not too disappointed. If by the end of my monastery tour, I believe Nada is the place, and if God wills it, a door will open—perhaps inviting a woman with family commitments might be a way that the community will reimagine itself. And so I tuck this little hermitage into a corner of my heart as I continue my search.

The morning I leave Nada, Kay brings me a card on which she's written the psalms from the office of that day:

> No more shall men call you "Forsaken,"
> Or your land "Desolate,"
> But you shall be called "My Delight,"
> And your land "Espoused."
> For the Lord delights in you,
> And makes your land his spouse.
>
> As a young man marries a virgin,
> Your Builder shall marry you;
> And as a bridegroom rejoices in his bride
> So shall your God rejoice in you.
>
> Isaiah 62:4–5

Midwifed

"Blessed Advent, my dear," the holiest woman I know, Estrella, effuses, taking both my hands and squeezing them in the lobby of a Ramada Inn, in Columbia, Missouri, where we had not planned on meeting. Due to forces beyond our control (God?), a blizzard has prevented me from spending a night with Estrella's friends, a group of elderly Benedictine nuns in the last gasps of keeping their monastery afloat, and I've been thrust upon her family, to celebrate her sister's fiftieth birthday in a banquet room.

Immediately I sense Christ's saying "Prophets are not without honor except in their own . . . homes" playing itself out. Estrella's family thinks she's strange. She's a self-professed hermit nun living in woods she calls the Holy Land, where women gather at ceremonies and run around without their shirts, cover themselves in mud from the creek, drum around the fire, howl at the moon.

Since I'm earlier than most of the guests, I help set up, filling and placing baskets of chips next to bowls of dip. I'm looking forward to getting to know Estrella's mother, Alida, who is relaxing at a corner table, watching. I've heard she's mean as a rattlesnake, a nightmare mother who planned her tortures. Yet since turning seventy, she'd been trying to turn a new leaf. "You're lucky," she'd told Estrella. "Kindness always came natural to you. Some of us have to work at it, hard. And you better believe it ain't easy."

I could relate. I had to babysit my sisters every weeknight in high school while my mother worked at the department store, and I would make my eight-year-old sister stand on the cellar stairs with the lights off and the door shut. Once I pulled a knife on my thirteen-year-old sister because she wanted to dry the dishes instead of wash, and I wanted to, too. I'm curious to see what a kindred spirit's new leaf looks like.

As I place a bowl of tortilla chips in front of Alida, she says, "Don't you hate helping?" To which I respond, "I like to help; it makes me feel useful."

"Really," she says, giving me the old fish eye, sizing me up, not believing a word.

It's the same old fish eye I'd used myself in Mexico the first time I met Estrella. Twenty-two of us were sipping lemonade on a veranda, awaiting an orientation for a fifty-four-mile pilgrimage to a miraculous Virgin. We were due to leave the next day, and as the hostess's caged miniature monkeys and gigantic parrots screeched nearby, a woman the size of an eleven-year-old, with hair to her butt, appeared in front of me, stood on her toes, stared into my eyes three beats longer than was comfortable, and in a musical whispery way said, "I'm Sister Sandra Morningstar. You can call me Sister Estrella if you'd like." She paused for me to tell her my name, then nodded in a way that made you think she already knew it, and continued. "I'm so happy to meet you. It's wonderful you could come. The walk is going to be life changing, don't you think? A little gift I brought for you." She dropped into my palm a tiny angel to pin on the baseball cap I'd been given with the "San Miguel Walk" logo stitched above its bill. Then she placed a hand on her heart, smiled, and said,

"Blessings on you," before moving to the next person, performing the same greeting, all the way around the room.

I suspected the sincerity of anyone that happy to see twenty-one strangers, and I wasn't sure I liked the touchy-feely tone she was establishing. The adolescent still alive and kicking in me might have mimed gagging, while the more mature me realized I should withhold judgment, better yet, not have any judgment at all—but this was not possible.

The next day, after winding through fields of cacti for twenty-five miles on earth so hard and dry it might as well have been cement, my feet felt like I'd been walking on the sun. I knew of course that we Catholics believe suffering leads to redemption. It says it in the Apostles Creed, "Christ suffered, died, and was buried; on the third day he arose from the dead and ascended into heaven." Obviously in the most quotidian way, the end of suffering brings relief, even release. I was not at the time, however, concerned with any of this. At the time I simply complained loudly at the campsite about my blisters, and Estrella responded, "May I rub your feet with healing oil?"

No one had ever offered to rub my feet before.

Who *was* this woman? She led me into a cool, dark tent, poured onto her palm a dollop of oil she told me she'd made herself from herbs on her Holy Land, then crossed her legs, placed my right foot in her lap, and rubbed while I asked her questions. I found out she's a hermit nun in an order of one, a midwife who does missionary work in Mexico and the rest of the year lives on sixty ever-increasing acres in the Ozarks of Missouri, her Holy Land. She's a mother of three grown daughters, and she'd learned about herbs and their medicinal properties from her Cherokee grandmother, from whom she'd also learned about Catholic nuns. Estrella was two or three when she saw her first one, walking down the main street of her town. "Why are they dressed like that?" she'd asked her grandmother, who told her that they were nuns and their job was to do good deeds. "And that was it. That's what I wanted to be, a nun."

I told her I'd wanted to be a nun, too, but it was mainly for the outfit, and because I wanted to be as mysterious and scary— thus powerful—as they were. I'd also been drawn to the idea of living with women, having breathed more easily whenever my father and his temper were out of sight. The San Miguel Walk— which had hooked up for two and a half days with a nine-day pilgrimage more than three hundred years old—was a protest against, as well as a fund-raiser to prevent, domestic violence. And so it felt natural to share how both my parents hit me but I was afraid of my father, an Italian American with a Roman-candle temper, who'd slapped me when he caught me lying, or sneaking around with boys, and also to shut my smart mouth and teach me respect, which it didn't.

The story Estrella told me is worse. She'd been beaten by her stepfather, once so badly with a belt that she passed out. At twelve, she'd been raped by a drunk uncle. When she gave birth to her first daughter during the days when you still had to sub-mit to being strapped to the table in the delivery room, the expe-rience triggered the memory of her rapist uncle pinning down her arms, and she delivered her daughter, literally, two minutes later, to get the hell out of that room. With her next daughter she decided to give birth at home with her husband's help. That worked okay, but with her youngest daughter she devised a bet-ter way. She sat on a beanbag chair and tilted up her pelvis to lift the baby out herself. She became a midwife, an ardent advocate of, as well as activist for, natural home births, a nun, and one of the women who helped with the founding of the first midwifery school in Latin America, which is an arm of CASA, the organization for whose domestic violence program the walk had raised funds.

The next day, Estrella and I met on the path, and she set me off like a Roman candle myself. "I love hot flashes," she actually said. "It's like the ocean rolling through your body—you've no control. So powerful."

"Are you *nuts*?" I shouted. "They're like atomic bombs! I'd rather die than go through another one. They make me even meaner. Hormone replacement therapy saved my life. I've never been happier, more even-tempered, calmer, blemish-free, *thinner*. Menopause sucks."

"Wouldn't miss it for the world." Estrella stood her ground. "I've always looked forward to being old. How're you going to be a wise old crone if you don't choose wisely to get there?"

Although I have an aversion to the whole "croning" business—why embrace a negative image to promote something positive—I've mostly looked forward to being old, too. And so I began to ponder what Estrella had said.

In the miracle room at the Virgin's basilica, I knelt with Estrella as she pinned to the wall her petition for a teepee chapel, along with a picture of the spot on her Holy Land where she planned to erect it. Tradition has it that if you walk to the Virgin with a petition, she will grant it. I asked to become a wise woman. (It would take years for me to consider that the rape might be one of the ways I am meant to get there.)

On the bus ride back to San Miguel, we leaned into each other and held hands like schoolgirls. The collective hopeful force of the seven thousand people we'd walked among; the kindness we'd witnessed all along the way: people handing out oranges or bottles of water from the beds of their rusted old

pickups; brass bands striking a tune; the group of old church ladies (probably younger than I was, come to think of it) with plas-
tic flowers on their hats, singing off-key with gusto; all this
opened me up to really hear Estrella when she said, "We're the
elders now. The world needs wise women so badly."

"You can't be wise and on hormones?"

She smiled kindly.

My response: to blurt, "I'm giving up hormones." Then, hearing the words come out of my mouth, I figured I really should.

It feels like the next moment, but might have been as much
as an hour later, the walk's organizer took the seat across the
aisle and asked for the umpteenth time if I'd please agree to be
the walk's organizer the following year. And I, who am as orga-
nized as pebbles dumped on a driveway; I, who am the type of
person at whom a psychiatrist friend recently shouted, "You
don't know you have ADD???!!!!"—twice—agreed to it. It was
time to give back; it was time to contribute by doing something
good for the world.

Although we traded e-mails all year, that second pilgrimage,
in January 2006, would be the next time I'd see Estrella. And
that second pilgrimage would be the last time I'd see her before
I'd be raped six months later.

I called Estrella right after I'd been lit on fire at the Abbey of
Regina Laudis and suspected I was experiencing a call. Estrella
had been happy for me and not surprised at all. "Pray to God,
pray every day," she said. "Pray, 'Open the path and I'll walk
it.'" I called her after I was raped, too. Again she didn't seem
surprised, and she gave the same advice, "Pray, 'Open the path
and I will walk it,'" then added, "'Knock and the door will be
opened, ask and you shall receive, seek and you will find.'" This
Advent the path opened to the Holy Land.

What good is Christ being born of Mary
If he's not born of us?

Meister Eckhart

"Don't you love Advent?" Estrella says the evening after her sister's birthday party. We've driven two hours on icy roads, been ferried through the snow on a four-wheeler by her son-in-law, and are seated on cushions in front of the fire she just built in Rose Cottage. Her little woodland house is decorated in a way that makes me expect to see doilies here and there. She lights a candle on the floor in front of us and says, "Christ is born in every one of us. Such a mystery, don't you think? I think advent is an invitation to open up more to Christ. What do you think?"

"I think Christ's coming, his being born, is an invitation to tap into the Christ spirit, the God spirit in us and maybe in the world, too—to access it."

"I think so, too."

Estrella looks as tired as I feel, so I politely refuse her offer of tea and trudge a fifteen-foot path in snow up to my knees from her cottage to mine. I will live in Casita for two weeks before departing a week before Christmas to spend the holiday with my family. The tiny house is two rooms with a combined area twice that of my hermitage at Nada. Casita was designed for people to stay in for short healing retreats. Furnishings are spare: The main room has a mobile-home-sized refrigerator, a microwave, a small desk, and a rocking chair; the bedroom has only a single bed; but the bathroom is luxuriously appointed with a sauna and a whirlpool tub.

Both houses and a tiny wooden chapel are nestled at the edge of the woods, facing gardens and a long meadow that gracefully slopes a long ways to the dirt road. In the middle of the meadow is the teepee chapel Estrella had prayed for on our first pilgrimage. Appearing to be walking out of the woods near a stream is a Mary statue Estrella rescued from a demolished church. Mary, dressed in periwinkle and white, is probably only four feet tall but seems life-sized, and her presence gives me comfort. It would be an exaggeration to say I feel safe here. But it's not an exaggeration to say I feel safer.

There is no TV or radio, or meat to eat on the Holy Land. But in Estrella's Rose Cottage there is a phone that hardly stops ringing: People she knows and people she's never met call to request prayers, schedule a time for a talk, ask for help. She's retired from being an active midwife and does soul work now. Her altar is crowded with people's pictures and petitions, candles, incense, a picture of Mary, a statue of Buddha. She bows, prays, lights candles, kneels. A community of young and not-so-young mothers and their children gather on the Holy Land for ceremonies through the year: full moon, equinox, solstice, yoga, wild women retreats, garden days. She has hung on a line between two trees the pictures of infants that died in childbirth. She prays daily "feminine rosaries" for pregnant women, inserting their names, "Hail, Jessica, full of grace, the Lord is with you . . ."

One day at dinner she tells me that lately so many people have been calling with news of unexpected deaths. "Will you pray for a young father?" she asks. "He has two small children, and his wife just died in childbirth. He hadn't wanted the child."

"The pain," I said, feeling it sinking my chest. "The guilt."

"Yes." She nods, placing a hand on her heart.

I observe that she does not turn from the pain, but it doesn't weigh her down, either. She accepts it as part of life, not to be embraced, perhaps, but to be integrated.

Estrella normally has little interaction with her retreatants, but for me, she says, she's making an exception. She invites me to pray vespers nightly with her in Rose Cottage, followed by meals, when I'm encouraged to share my thoughts and feelings, what's happening inside, my nightly dreams, to discuss anything that comes up, anything at all. "It's my greatest wish," she says, "to help with your spiritual discernment."

I tell her about waking up scared in the middle of so many nights.

"Yes." She nods, as though she already knew.

"Why rape?" I ask. "What am I supposed to learn?"

She smiles.

Years later, when I'm writing this book, she will tell me that I was easily startled and my eyes darted around. She will try to remind me of an incident I still don't remember. A group of women had gathered for a day on the Holy Land while I was there. One of the women, mourning a stillbirth, had gone down by the creek to scream. Hearing her, I barreled out of the bathroom, my pants around my ankles, shouting in outrage, "There's a predator on the HOLY LAND!!!???"

Every day, to be a nun or not to be a nun is the question I can't shake, or answer. Eventually, this question conflates with the wish Estrella told me she makes at each newborn's birth while lifting them up to the heavens, "May you live long enough to know why you were born." This seems another way of stating my ambition: to be who God meant me to be.

"Before you go to sleep," Estrella counsels, "ask God what She wants you to know."

I dream that I'm caring for a baby I've neglected and left all alone. I change its dirty diaper and feed it a bottle of milk.

"It's God," Estrella tells me.

I dream there's a stick in my salad. When I poke at it, it turns into a regal bejeweled praying mantis, wearing a diamond crown above a cute Betty Boop face.

"That's you," Estrella says. "God made you a peacock. Somehow you'll use that."

Can I be a peacock and a nun, too? Could I ever in my entire life become a person able to give and to love one half of one percent as much as Christ did, or for that matter, as Estrella does?

God doesn't love you because you're good.
God loves you because God is good.

Many People

When she was a little girl, Estrella looked at a couple of nuns and thought, I want to be kind like they are; I looked at nuns and thought I want to be mean like they are. Christ talks about having "eyes to see" and "ears to hear." My eyes looked and saw the underbelly, the fallen, the hurt and suffering, who mostly didn't know they were hurt and suffering. Not so I could help them like Christ or Mother Teresa but because I found them as interesting as a Dickens novel. I think I believed they were my tribe, my birds of a feather, like I recognized a tribe member in Estrella's mother—and maybe they were. Like many of them, I didn't know I was hurt and suffering. I thought I was bad news, lazy, depressed, and looking for a little fun—also known as happiness—however I could find it, almost always in darkness: I get a scholarship to a fantastic, life-changing university, graduate, and head immediately to New York with no job and a ten-year-old kid. It's in my first apartment in Little Italy where I look out my window and hear the little old Italian sisters in the window above mine say, "Is that Johnny?"

"No."

"Yeah, yeah, it's Johnny, Lena's boy."

I watched as Johnny got hammered on the head by a cop with a blackjack before falling nose first onto the hood of a car and slithering to the ground.

On a wire across the road from telephone pole to telephone pole a banner hung, with the words "Pimps, Whores, Johns, Go Home." I wrote this in my notebook. I thought it all romantic. I thought I'd finally arrived. When I was a kid my favorite show was *The Naked City.* "There are eight million stories in the Naked City," the narrator would intone after each episode. "This has been one of them." My favorite episode featured a murder during which all the people in the building heard the screams and did nothing.

People walked around my Naked City with pissed pants, they slept in refrigerator boxes. I moved to Alphabet City, but it could have been called Crack Depot, Junkie Haven, Hello Hell. My landlady's boyfriend was stabbed under my window. Men fought using garbage can lids as shields. Once, in front of me, a man knocked a grocery bag out of a woman's hands, and as she bent to pick up the eggplant rolling in the gutter, he yelled, "And f— your f—ing eggplant." I was appalled. I wrote it down. When I told the story to people, I laughed.

This was real life. This was material. And this, I believed, would make *me* interesting. *Nice?* Don't even say the word; you'll make me fall asleep.

What was that song: "Accentuate the positive and eliminate the negative"?

A contrarian to the bone, I did the opposite.

A loud part of me looks myself in the eye and says, "How dare you?" You upstart prodigal daughter, reading saints and mystics, you Johnny-come-lately, who the hell do you think you are?

Estrella transformed her own painful experience in childbirth to minister to other pregnant women and to advocate for safer, loving home births.

Now, post-rape, I'm hoping to transform the pain, to take the nasty thing that happened to me and make it into something good. Maybe by writing about it one day. But at the moment, it's more important to live what I am living than to document it. I want this experience to be pure, felt, in the moment. So I write about what's happening only when I will burst if I don't—which turns out to be fairly often.

I satisfy the writing urge—or is it an addiction?—by working for a few hours each day on a rewrite of a middle-grade novel, which my editor is awaiting.

Almost a decade before my visit, Estrella wrote her own vows. I've been wondering what my vows would be if I wrote my own, too. One evening, when I've only a few days left to my stay, I write them out:

Constant Prayer

I vow to pray with my heart and my mind,
In work and in leisure, in stillness and movement,
Inviting God as the focus of my days and nights.

Chastity

I vow to be chaste in body and mind, fasting from
Sex, criticisms, judgments, fear and worry,
So that I may love more fully every person, animal,
    deed, and event that crosses my path.

Silence

I vow to observe silence to
Feel my heart,

Be led by the spirit,
And hear God whenever s/he calls.

I finish late in the evening, and in the morning when I read them over, my chest feels so full it hurts. I cry for a half hour during which I realize I want these vows to be true.

Then I wonder, Why can't I make these promises, live as a nun for a year, and then see?

Estrella is thrilled. She calls me Sister Bev, she blesses my vows in a communion service, and then requests a copy to keep on her altar so she can pray for them and me. In my best handwriting, I print them onto a lovely card decorated with pressed yellow pansies, which I'd bought in the Snowmass gift shop. She suggests I accompany her on her monthly visit to her spiritual director, Father Paul, so he can bless them, too, and I happily agree.

> Teach your mouth to say
> That which you have in your heart.
>
> Abba Poeman, Desert Father

We drive an hour and arrive in time for dinner, which we order at a local roadside restaurant. The waitress is young, shy, overweight. She seems to want to dip her face into her shirt, perhaps because of acne that is so angry some of it has turned purple. Estrella beams at her. "How are you today? What's your name? It's so nice of you to serve us."

The young woman beams back. "My name's Kristin, but people call me Krissy. Just moved here a couple of months ago."

"That's why I never saw you here before. I'm Sister Morningstar and this is Sister Bev. I come here once a month, so now we know each other's names."

I start at being called Sister Bev.

"Yes, ma'am." She nods and blushes. "Used to be I knew everybody. I come from a small town, smaller than here."

I look at the menu, trying to think of something genuine and reassuring to say to her—to spread some love. Now that I'm a nun, I hope to, as much as I'm able, which means at least sometimes, remember to be kind to people. Being a nun is not going to be easy. Finally I think to say, "You're too friendly not to make friends," and I mean it.

Krissy smiles before dropping her eyes to her order pad.

The next morning Father Paul welcomes us in and makes a fire in the living area of his wood-paneled hermitage. He's thin as a sapling and nearly eighty years old. A Methodist minister for thirty years, he converted to Catholicism, became a Trappist priest, and then, seeking more solitude, a Trappist hermit. In a cedar forest, Father Paul has built his own cabin, and there is also a guesthouse, with a terrace overlooking a small lake. He has rigged his phone to chime for Lauds, Matins, Vespers, and Compline so he'll remember to stop and pray in the Office. He continues to write theological books, of which he has published a dozen.

When Father Paul finally sits, he doesn't say so much as bark at me, "So, you don't want to go through the accepted channels? You have problems with the Church?"

I hadn't expected this and am so nervous I spout rather than speak. Either I say all of what follows, or only some. I don't remember exactly, so rather than selecting, I'm recounting all of my opinions at the time: "I love the Church. I don't approve of some, well a lot of, the Church's stands on issues. I don't like the conservative direction in which I see it heading; I don't like the systemic denial; the sexual scandals, the immoral cover-ups; I don't like the male hierarchy; I do not believe the Pope is infallible; I think there should be women priests, married priests, birth control, homosexuals welcomed in the pews, but I'm as much a part of the Church as anybody. And if it has any chance of changing it'll only happen from the inside."

He nods encouragingly, and I relax while explaining further, "It's just that I don't know if I'm going to join a convent or a monastery, but I want to take vows and try to live up to them for a year. And see."

"Sounds like a good plan." He smiles and offers his hand, which I shake. We then have mass, seated in his living room around a cross section of a tree he uses as a coffee table. For the first reading, Father Paul hands me a psalm from that day's office. When I read the line "The Lord is kind and merciful, slow to anger and abounding in steadfast love," I choke up: this is how God *feels* to me. And this is how I want to be.

Before I leave the following day, Estrella tells me that if I decide the life of a religious is for me, I am welcome to join her, and we'll be an order of two. I imagine making enough money one day to build a cabin in the woods down by the creek. I am drawn to a community that includes so much contact with children. But I do not do well in the heat and I'm afraid I'll be rendered comatose by the hot, humid Missouri summers. And I'm not sure what I think of howling at the moon. Still, I'm grateful to have this invitation, and I feel a bit calmer, not so untethered. Now when I awake in the middle of the night with anxiety about a future I can't know, I remind myself that this holy place will have me.

Unpack My Bags

It's no fun when God is not near.

Hafiz

It's Christmas Eve, and I'm walking from my parents' house in Wallingford, Connecticut, to midnight mass at Holy Trinity Church. It's so warm it's almost balmy out, and I've been looking forward to being outside, silent, and alone for the half-mile stroll. As I walk, I think about how the church chose to celebrate Christ's birthday on one of the darkest days of the year, the moment before the balance tips and the light begins again to grow. The stars are out, and I feel as awestruck as I did when I was a kid, picturing Mary on a donkey, the three kings on camels following a star. I wonder if it's possible that shepherds really heard choirs of angels singing, and if so, how some would have felt frightened and others blessed.

I'm pleased with myself for resisting wine at dinner so I would not fall asleep like the rest of my family has—not that anyone would have accompanied me to church had they been awake. Only my mother believes in God. She, my youngest sister, Janet, with whom I'm close; and my son, Jason, are the only people in my family I've told about my becoming a nun. But one of them must have leaked it to my middle sister Pat's husband, Frank, because he'd brought it up at our Christmas Eve fish feast. We'd served ourselves spaghetti with anchovy sauce, stuffed sole, eel, shrimp smelts and were entertained by sixteen-month-old Zach, who was celebrating Christmas with the Donofrio clan for the first time. Frank, a.k.a. The Bomber, pointed a finger at him, " 'You better be good, you better not pout, you better not cry, I'm telling you why.' Why, Zachary?"

Zach lifted both arms like an ump announcing a field goal, and we shouted, "Santa!" We laughed, clapped, finished the song, then Frank turned to me. "Hey, Bev, what's this I hear, you're a nun now?"

I wanted to discuss this about as much as I want to discuss politics, which is approximately never. We do joke in my family, thankfully, but we don't share intimacies, and we avoid controversy like someone else's bad breath. Except for recipes, stories about little kids and about when we were kids—or anything to do with the Yankees—nobody's interested. Tonight, though, Frank is curious.

"Only for a year," I answer. "Then I'll see."

"Then what? You won't be a nun anymore?"

"It's like an engagement. Maybe I will and maybe I won't."

"So it's official, this is a real thing?"

"Well, not to the Church. It's official to me."

"That's why you're not dressed like a nun?"

I considered explaining that since Vatican II a lot of nuns have elected not to wear habits, choosing instead to dress as common people, which was what habits once were: the dress of the masses. But instead, on impulse, I said, "Just call me Sister Bev."

"You're serious?" My son's eyes grew.

I changed the subject. "Where's Santa, Zach?"

Zach shook his head, saying, "Ah no," his version of "I don't know."

"Is he heading from the North Pole in his sleigh?" I ask. "Who's pulling Santa's sleigh?" Thus inciting a welcomed diversionary eruption of "Rudolf the Red-nosed Reindeer."

At the end of my parents' road, I take a left onto Route 5, and Holy Trinity's a straight shot down the highway. Across the road behind a stone wall is the graveyard, where my great-grandparents and their eldest daughter, born in Italy, are buried. The only one alive when I was born was my great-grandmother Irene, who spoke an English I could barely understand, had hair white as cotton and legs thick as young-tree stumps standing a foot apart. Greatgrammy was a walker like I am. Until we moved when I was nearly five, we'd often run into her on this stretch near the cemetery. I'd be holding on to the side of the carriage handle as my mother pushed my sister Pat and my brother, Ed, walked ahead. Greatgrammy would work her black change purse out of her pocket, then with short, thick fingers fish out a lint-covered penny or Life Saver to press into my palm. I said thank you, as I knew I should, but longed to hide my face between my mother's legs until we went on our way, or Greatgrammy did. She spoke and smelled funny, and I didn't see her often enough to get used to her. With fingers that were hard and dry and barely touching, she'd lift my chin to see my face. If I were brave that day, I'd look into her eyes and see merriment there. I knew I was the reason for that look in her eyes, and I'd want her to stay and come along with us; yet I dreaded this, too.

She was my father's grandmother and, as my mother described it, had once been "well-to-do." Her husband had been a major in the Italian army, and in the States he made and displayed fireworks, a lucrative business at the time. But my great-grandmother was generous and foolhardy, and when he died it didn't take her long to spend or give away every penny. Some she gave to the Church. My mother would say with bitterness that my great-grandmother had crocheted the doilies they used on the altar but, in the end, she didn't attend church because she couldn't afford the quarter to put in the basket, and was too ashamed. I always believed this, until tonight. Maybe Greatgrammy didn't need to go to church to commune with God. Maybe she'd rather be out walking on a Sunday morning. Maybe my mother was projecting.

My mother claimed that the reason she herself never attended church or took us children, except for on holidays, was because she couldn't afford a decent hat or a nice coat. I used to believe that, too. My mother was second-generation Italian American, the "daughter of a ditch digger," as she used to say. She felt poor, low class, and disrespected. The Church of her day was run by the Irish, fair, blue-eyed, native English-speakers whose ancestors had staked their claims generations before my mother's. Yet even if you're socially comfortable, it's easy to make excuses not to attend church—and if it doesn't feed you, maybe then you shouldn't go. I remember those old days back in the fifties, when the priest intoned homilies in a droning, sing-songy Latinate-sounding speech, the same way he delivered the gospel. He'd tell us we were wicked, silly, sinful, then shake his head in disgust at the money we were not coughing up, the money that presumably would buy us the love of God—which was rarely if ever mentioned, and to me seems the whole point.

Back then, we were told that if you missed church on Sunday you'd burn in hell. Today, it's hard to understand how the Church can forbid the use of condoms even when a spouse has AIDS, and how it won't allow innocuous gluten-free hosts to people suffering from celiac disease—who can eat the gluten in wheat only at certain peril to their health—because canon law states that the holy Eucharist must be made of wheat and water. The Church can seem like it's run by modern-day Pharisees, the enforcers of rules and sticklers for the law, whom Jesus called "hypocrites, whose teachings are but rules taught by men." Fundamentalists are the scourge of every religion.

Yet the monastery, hermitage, retreat centers I had just visited as well as the ones I was about to visit, would not exist without the Church. Monks wouldn't gather in the chapel in the middle of the night to pray for the poor and the lonely and the lost; there would be no nuns in beat-up jeeps bumping through jungles and city streets to minister to refugees, no nuns running homeless and battered-women shelters, orphanages, safe houses. There'd be no priests and nuns organizing soup kitchens and food pantries, ministering to the sick, the dying, the abandoned, the condemned. No more of this powerful organization's lobbying to abolish the death penalty.

And no churches, silent as eternity, to sit or kneel or smell incense in, light a candle, sit under the gaze of saints making mysterious gestures in stained-glass windows, Christ above on a cross, Mary in a statue looking down. "I like the silent church," Emerson wrote, "before the service begins." I'd have had no holy place to drop into to recollect myself, touch base with my soul, my feelings, to look for that something deeper below my thoughts, no holy place to wheel Zach into whenever I visit Brooklyn.

On walks, Zach and I drop in for a few minutes and sometimes for services. One Sunday, when he was just under a year, we took a seat up front at Assumption of the Blessed Virgin Mary church, where he fell promptly to sleep. Rather than disturb him when the mass ended, I remained in my seat, as did half the congregation, for some sort of celebration. More people streamed in until the church was nearly full, and when the priest began to speak I realized it was the fiftieth anniversary of a nun's vows. The priest recounted the woman's accomplishments: soup kitchens and homeless shelters she'd founded and run, and an orphanage in Africa.

Then the nun stood. She was slim and dressed in a polyester, flower-printed, shirtwaist dress from another decade and walked to the area in front of the altar in her stockings. She lifted herself onto her toes, threw her arms wide, and began a dance to recorded swelling, orchestral music. I will later hear that what she performed is called "liturgical dance." It seemed improvised and all about her heart lifting to God. I couldn't stop my sense of aesthetics, my ex–New Yorker artiness from flinching at the corniness, nor could I stop my heart from exclaiming, Wow. Look at her! This woman was at least in her seventies, and so alive, expressive, and brave. And look at all she'd accomplished.

The larger world of celebrity, public awards, and accolades does not register what this nun or people like her do, people who might number in the tens or hundreds of thousands for all I know.

Seated in the church were family and friends this nun had left. Her leaving may have been a process, at the end of which she could ignore the call no longer, and had done as Christ asked, "Leave your father and mother . . . Let the dead bury the dead . . . Keep your hand on the plow and do not look back . . . Sell what you own, give the money to the poor and come and follow me"

Christ is a master storyteller, who exaggerates to make a point. It's doubtful he meant that we literally must leave the dead to bury the dead; it's possible the phrase was a colloquialism. He's saying the life of the spirit, your relationship with God, must come first. "The Kingdom of God is like a treasure buried in a field, which a man found and covered up; then in his joy he goes and sells all that he has to buy that field." This wasn't talk about heaven once you're dead; it's talk about heaven right now.

I take a seat up front. "Thank you for this church," I say. "And for its priests, for Christ being born of Mary to be born of me, for the growing of the light."

Through Nature

Days are Gods,
Each one laden with gifts
We are never quite able to take.

Ralph Waldo Emerson

I'm at the Desert House of Prayer in Tucson, Arizona. It's sunny and warm and January. But in the mornings on my way to Lauds and mass in the chapel, it's still dark and winter cold. I walk on sand and pebbles past saguaros and prickly cacti, then sit in the chapel on a folding chair in a line of them, facing another line of them. It's high season, so most of the twenty or so chairs are filled with retreatants, and also the four religious who run the place. Twice a day, at Lauds and Vespers, we chant in haunting melodies led by Sister Jenny, whose voice is resonant as wind chimes.

After the morning services, I make myself a breakfast of cereal with bananas and green grapes, then eat, warmed by the roaring fire in the living room. But just as often, I sit in the kitchen in front of a sliding-glass door to watch birds rioting at a flat-tray bird feeder. It hangs from an old paloverde a few feet away, and I'm most fascinated by the king of the birds, a red cardinal as wide as a sumo wrestler and as long as my size-nine foot. He eats all he wants and for a long time, because the others grant him a wide berth.

Then one day the cardinal doesn't appear. For days, I look for him every morning, I hunt for him everywhere I walk, I wonder about him in the middle of the night. And when he stays missing for a whole week, I accept that he has to be dead. I want to believe that if his end was violent he'd been given the grace of shock, like I had when at thirty-three I was hit by a car, crossing Thirty-fourth Street in Manhattan. I forgot it was two-way, looked one way, stepped into the street, and was slammed in the hip. I flew through the air calm as a leaf and landed on the asphalt the same way. I'd felt not a pinch of pain until hours later, after I was released from the emergency room and in the cab headed home. The day after I was raped, after not sleeping a wink, I ran around town with the energy of a two-year-old, doing errands I'd postponed for months. Each time I ran into someone I knew I'd say, "Hey, how're you? Oh, by the way, I was raped last night. It's okay. I'm fine. Really."

My friend Dave was hit in the bum by a car going seventy miles an hour and declared dead. He says *peaceful* doesn't begin to describe the bliss he felt. He saw his body twisted on the side of the highway, emergency workers bending over him. He heard what they were saying, knew what they were thinking. Simultaneously, he was presented with a newsreel of his life, while feeling deeply peaceful and accepting of it all, possessed of an understanding that everything was as it should be. His body flowed down a tunnel of light, toward brighter light, with no sense of time because there was no time, and suddenly he was back in his broken, aching body on the side of the highway. Dave has never felt one iota of fear about dying since.

I've one friend who thinks I'm a Christian because I'm so

desperate to believe in an afterlife, I'm willing to believe a myth—that Jesus is the son of God sent to die in reparation for Adam's sin of disobedience. Which then opened the gates of heaven and gave us eternal life. The only part of that dogma I believe is that Jesus is the son of God. I believe lots of things that have nothing to do with the myth: reincarnation and karmic law to name a couple.

I refuse to believe that God punished the whole race for Adam's sin, or that God punishes—ever. We choose heaven or hell every day, every moment, of our lives.

One day I heard a man whistling outside my hermitage and became frightened and then enraged that he'd ruined my illusion of solitude and safety: hell. One day alone in the wilderness, I heard someone playing a flute in a cave and lifted onto my toes to get nearer to it: heaven.

While hiking every day, I try to do as Evelyn Underhill described in her illuminating little book *Practical Mysticism*. I think about being united to the natural, the spiritual, and the divine, hoping to experience them as one. Hoping that by observing with a "contemplative eye," I will see things for their own sake. Going beyond the "vision of common sense," I will "see with eyes of love," in "disinterested adoration."

I keep up my disciplines, meditating three times a day, prayer in chapel, hours of spiritual reading, and like Brother Lawrence, I try to hold a running conversation with God, throwing up little thank-yous all the time.

> God wants us to allow ourselves to see God continually,
> for God wants to be seen and wants to be sought.
> God wants to be awaited and wants to be trusted.
>
> Julian of Norwich

I had never thought of God in a two-way relationship, never imagined God as needing anything, never thought God would desire my love.

Mystics and theologians say that one way to love God is to love the things God created, and as I hike through Saguaro National Park, which is only a stone's throw away, I say, "Look at what you made!" I notice how every pebble under my foot is different from every other pebble—and how this must be true of every pebble, grain of sand, cell in the world. I recite my memorized prayers, sometimes I say a rosary, and in this way I make my walks through the wilderness a constant prayer—at least I do for stretches when my mind isn't running amok. I am awed by mountain lion tracks and laugh when I finally spot a small herd of grunting javelinas. Deer stop and look at me, roadrunners hurry on their way, hawks glide in the sun-bleached sky, and one day a lizard darts across my path. I stop, and the lizard stops, too, motionless at the edge of the wash, still as stone, in front of a boulder.

I wonder if it stopped so I could pay attention to it. If God stopped it for me. It reminds me of alligators and dinosaurs, dragons and the frogs boys in elementary school used to chase me with; it's deeply strange, probably prehistoric, and to someone who's never dared touch a frog, creepy.

I've an urge to poke it with a stick, not to hurt it, just to slide the stick under its belly, to see if it can jump, to watch how it moves.

Maybe the lizard stopped not only so I could get a better look at it, but so it could get a better look at me.

I have read what I believe to be true: war, burglary, rape are actions that treat the other as an object. All violence treats the other as an object. St. Teresa heard God's voice saying, "Seek yourself in me, and in yourself seek me." Maybe God is both other and inside you and me and all things, including this creature. We are all in God. This reptile is in God. By poking the lizard I'd be making an "object" of it, forcing it to react to, to run away from, me. So I imagine my heart filling with love, imagine that this love is the same God-love that's inside the lizard.

I notice it has an astonishing pattern of green and yellow diamonds on its back, like a lizard harlequin.

How could I not have noticed this before?

This sort of thing has happened before. In San Miguel, I went on an outing with a group of bird-watchers through the botanical preserve above the town. When the leader spotted a hawk on a narrow ledge of the canyon wall, he set up his telescope on a tripod and invited us all to look. I stared through that telescope for a full two minutes before I could separate the bird from the wall. The hawk was huge and obvious and impossible to miss. Yet I'd missed it.

I tired of bird-watching and headed out alone, back toward home along the path I'd walked, weather and spirits permitting, a few times a week for years. As I reached the highest elevation, up above me on the top branch of a dead tree, perched an enormous bird, taller than the hawk I'd just seen, its breast feathers cloud white and fluttering in the breeze. If it knew of my presence, it ignored it, gazing into the distance, calm as dawn, its beak hooked like an owl's. I filled with awe barely this side of fear. I was certain God had put the bird there to teach me something. I knew I had noticed this magnificent bird only as a result of having seen the other bird minutes before. The one sighting had opened my eyes for another. Christ said, "Let those with eyes to see, see." I wondered what else, plain as the nose on my face, I constantly miss.

St. Paul said, "When I'm weak I'm strong."

+ + +

Maybe the rape has made me weak enough to be strong enough
to see something I've been blind to.

One summer when I was eight or nine or ten, I trapped the little
boy next door under a heavy iron lawn chair. I tipped it over on
top of him, making a jail. He'd play along for a while, but when I
wouldn't release him, he'd get upset, which was what I'd trapped
him for. The urge I had to make him cry was lustful—almost
sexual, certainly physical. I'd held the boy captive, taken away
his will, forced him to submit to mine and to beg in tears. My
pleasure was dependent on my own cruelty and his tears. This is
called sadism. I have been sadistic. I have done evil. I have been
evil.

The rapist must have had a similar urge. The ex–FBI agent
said the rapist possessed low self-esteem, that he needed to rape
to feel powerful. Exerting our will over others makes us feel
powerful.

Could the rapist have resisted the urge?

Could I have?

> A characteristic of sin:
> The person is held captive by the love
> For what he knows he should hate.
>
> Thomas Merton

By the tenth grade a favorite pastime was to sit in front of the
mirror, imagining an angel on one shoulder and a devil on the
other. The angel told me to be kind and good and helpful, like a
girl scout. The devil told me to gossip and lie, lure others into
trouble, like a villain. I lied to get out of trouble, get off the hook,

get going. I lied to give an impression, usually bad: "I was raised on a chicken farm, my brother shot my father, and my mother burned the coops down." I gossiped, told secrets, turned friends against each other, and closer to me. At a dinner party a few years ago in San Miguel a woman said, "I've never understood how people think being cruel can make them happy. I've always been kind, because I understood that being otherwise would backfire."

Why did I enjoy looking in the mirror and imagining the devil behind my eyes staring back?

Christ chased a lot of demons out of a lot of people. I sure hope loving him is chasing the demons out of me.

One way to love God is to love even our torturers. Even ourselves.

I sit cross-legged in the wash to be more comfortable, and the lizard still doesn't run away. The harlequin lizard I see now is stunningly beautiful. And I tell it so. "You are gorgeous," I whisper. "Thank you for letting me look at you.

"And thank you, God, for making our paths cross."

I wonder: If you take the time to really look at anything will it become beautiful?

It's two weeks since the cardinal disappeared. One morning, I'm walking by the sliding glass doors, and I see him. It seems impossible; I don't at first trust my eyes. But there's no doubt it's him, thinner—and *missing his tail*.

He sits on a low branch of a smaller paloverde tree five feet behind the larger one while the other birds eat. Only after they've all flown off does he drop to the ground and hop over to scavenge through their leavings in the dirt.

Has he been starving somewhere, half dead? Now every morsel of food will be a struggle. He's weak and has no defenses; he can't fly away. He could be devoured by one of those piggy javelinas. He'd be better off dead. This diminishment, this tragedy is the way of the world, common as milk. One day, you have your health and well-being, and the next you've lost your job, child, spouse, lung, friend; you've been beaten up, slandered, destroyed, raped. What you assumed, presumed, planned on one moment is in the next moment stolen away—not possible.

Maybe a radical disruption followed by diminishment, or just the slow accretion of losses we experience over a lifetime, is God's way of preparing us for death. Maybe it's God's way of loosening our attachment to life by leaving us less and less to cling to.

I am not comforted by this thought.

Back in my hermitage, I cry for the bird, and then I cry for me. Less than before: afraid of the dark; a scared little mouse hiding away in monasteries, adoring silence because I've been stunned dumb. I'm old and gray and want my beautiful black hair back. I want every dead pet, a bluesy saxophone on a sultry night, a man's hand on my thigh. My friends and I shouting at a bar, playing pool, dancing to the jukebox. Done, over, gone, no second chance, no reset, no revisit.

After the rape, one of the rapist's other victims sent me the gift of an energy worker, who said it's a miracle that I could even stand. "Your adrenals are completely drained. You have *no* energy."

All that running around town the day after the rape had been done on fumes. At my age can adrenals recover?

Is it even possible to change?

All this talk about becoming who God wants me to be. Isn't it a bit late for that? Haven't I squandered my chances? Isn't my nature hardwired, hasn't my personality atrophied? "You can't teach an old dog new tricks" mocks me like a schoolyard taunt.

> The path to wisdom is through
> Suffering, failure, loss,
> Not security.
>
> Practically every sage ever born

Then like the marines on Iwo Jima, God sends me Sisters Helen and Marla. Sister Helen has trumped my age by a decade and a half. She's taking advantage of having to be in town for a job interview as a drug rehabilitation counselor by making a retreat at Desert House. Sister Helen has been a teacher, social worker, psychotherapist, lecturer, and workshop leader on women's empowerment issues. Her last job, as a drug rehabilitation counselor, had been at the Betty Ford Clinic, which she left to perform a two-year stint in leadership at her motherhouse.

I found this out by sitting next to her at one of two large round tables in the living-dining area. (Dinnertime is the only time speaking in public spaces is allowed.) After the first dinner, we make sure to sit next to each other. One evening she surprises me by showing up with chestnut brown hair. Just that morning it had been salt and pepper. "Nobody wants to hire an old lady," she says. "Because they're too stupid to know better."

Then Sister Marla—a young, robust, apple-cheeked blonde, who looks like she just came down from climbing an alp— arrives. She lives in a house in the woods in Wisconsin and basically acts as the pastor of her church, in a rural area where men priests are too few. Because no one but a priest is allowed to change bread and wine into the body and blood of Christ, she conducts what's called a communion service, during which she reads the gospel and delivers the homily. A priest comes on Sundays to say mass and bless enough hosts to last until he returns. For every other day of the week, Marla teaches, prays with the dying, visits people in the hospital and at home, counsels, and I've no doubt makes a fine priest. She's smart as a whip and cracks me up. I crack Marla up. Ellen cracks us both up. One evening we can't stop and remain at table long after everyone else has left—talking in public spaces until after midnight.

Because I'm exhausted from laughing, I sleep through the night for the first time since the rape.

The next morning when I wake up late and have to rush to Lauds, I consider wearing my pajamas to give my new girlfriends a laugh. Then as I hurry in the dark to the chapel, this occurs to me: Didn't Christ come to earth to teach even old dogs new tricks?

It is not God's will
That we pine and mourn
Over feelings of pain,
But that we get better
And continue to enjoy life.

Julian of Norwich

A few days before I leave, I look out the sliding glass doors and see a miracle: The cardinal is growing a new tail.

The religious who run Desert House of Prayer are from different orders, on assignment from their individual communities. There is also Margaret, a lay woman in her late sixties, who is a widow and grandmother. She'd come on retreat and asked if she could live here for six months a year, and help out, mainly in the office, booking retreatants. The residents each perform a job here but do not together form a community. So there is nothing to really join. I consider that wherever I land I might be like Margaret, a lay woman, living on site, helping out.

Unless Margaret were to leave, there doesn't seem to be a position like that here. But I find some comfort in the knowledge that if I should like to return, I could always come for $1,500 a month, my own hermitage, sung prayer in the chapel, the Saguaro National Forest—meals included.

Paradise Lost

If you comprehend it, it is not God.

St. Augustine

I have come to Sand Springs, Oklahoma, to Osage Benedictine Monastery, the last stop on my pilgrimage. Osage is nestled into forty-five wooded acres called the Forest of Peace, and during the month of my stay, I live in my own small, wooden-box-like cabin in the woods. So do a few other retreatants who come and go; a woman masseuse, who is interning for a year; and six nuns. One, a Dominican with the physicality of a football player, is visiting for a year and probably in her late forties; another is my age; and the other four are so old their feet snap like kindling as they enter the round chapel in stocking feet each morning, noon, and afternoon for prayer. The oldest, Sister Priscilla, celebrated her ninetieth birthday this year, for which a celebratory DVD was made. Accompanied by "Flight of the Bumble Bee," we see wispy thin Priscilla in the chapel beating each pillow, dusting, vacuuming, watering the plants; then racing to the main house, where she vacuums again, washes and dries dishes, wipes down counters, mops the floor, sets the table, waters plants, sews on a sewing machine. I am told that she arrived here with the founder, Sister Pascaline, in the seventies, and will leave only when Pascaline does, or in a coffin. I wonder if for all these years she's made work a constant prayer, as St. Benedict intended. I wonder if this ninety-year-old's energy comes from the Holy Spirit— and what spirit-fueled activities the other nuns are up to all day.

I soon realize that one thing they're up to is cooking. Everyone's on their own for breakfasts, a cook prepares weekday lunches, but all the meals are shopped for by the nuns, and all dinners and weekend lunches are prepared by them—for as many as a dozen or more at a sitting. The nuns basically put on a dinner party every day. No wonder they never smile. (A meal with strangers once a week, like at Nada's Sunday brunches, is more my speed.) Following their rule, to treat every stranger as Christ, may have taken its toll on these sisters. Or maybe a life of prayer has made them so comfortable with who they are, they can be happy without the need to show anybody signs of happiness. But then I must also consider the obvious: They simply may be unhappy or even depressed.

(I had no way of knowing at the time that I was mistaking sadness for depression, even bitterness. The sisters' days of living at the Forest of Peace were numbered, they knew it, and could not mention it. Their larger community is aging and shrinking, and could no longer support running the place. Osage would pass into other hands, and the sisters, some who'd thought they would die at Osage, would be transferred, most of them back to the motherhouse.)

Sister Pascaline is different. She may not smile much, but it's obvious she's in her element. (And I never see her cook.) She runs some arm of the Bede Griffiths foundation in her own office and meets with a stream of people who come for spiritual direction. Forty years ago, a visit to Griffiths's monastery in India, which blended Eastern and Western spiritual practices, had inspired Pascaline to found Osage, where the chapel is sunken and round and you may sit on a floor cushion, at a kneeler, or in a chair when you meditate with the group before services. Readings during prayer services are chosen from many traditions, not only Christian. (This had been true of the readings at Nada, too.) Pascaline is now in her seventies, with a man's handsome face and eyes too dark to be warm, eyes you might avoid if you're afraid of being seen through. At the moment, Sister Pascaline is not the abbess, benign Sister Benita is, although you'd never know it. Pascaline seems to have the first and the last word, and when she enters a room, I feel like I should jump to my feet as I'd done for the Mother Superior at catechism, shouting, "Good afternoon, Sister."

At dinner one night Sister Pascaline incites a short exchange that rattles me like a house in a hurricane. She's seated at the end of the long dining table where I can't see her. Across from me in the middle of the table is Sister Sarah, the sister who is my age and a convert from Judaism. Sister Pascaline says in a tone so assertive it presents as indisputable fact, or the *Baltimore Catechism*: "God can prevent anything from happening. So if it happened, it's God's will." And Sarah, who has recently returned from a seminar in Chicago, responds that there's no such word as *omnipotence* in Hebrew. *Omnipotence* comes from the Greek. The omnipotent or "All Powerful" God derived from the Greek translation of the Hebrew word for "hosts" into "armies." But that definition was rarely used, and it probably should have been translated into a "Host of Angels." At the seminar, impressive arguments were presented to suggest that God can and does change.

This discussion sends me into such a fit of anxiety, I do not remember and perhaps never even hear how Sister Pascaline responds. If God is not only *not* all powerful, but changeable, in process, learning, and not perfect, God may have no way of even influencing let alone determining what happens to anyone.

When I called Father Friehl after the rape, he'd said that God would never cause evil but God will use it. I suspect that Father Friehl would agree with Sister Pascaline, that if God had wanted to prevent the rape, God would have. This I can take (I think).

But prayer did chase the rapist out, didn't it? Or was it my own cunning, banking on the rapist's having at least a remnant of belief, banking on his guilt. If God has no agency, no power to make manifest anything in this world, then prayers are futile, and we have no recourse for help. I will not be able to calm myself with "Your will, not mine," accepting the vagaries of life while having faith that beyond my knowledge or imagining, pain and disappointment have some meaning or lesson I cannot at the moment, or even in this lifetime, understand. But if God can't influence what happens in this world, then when bad things happen, when disappointments occur, they are just that: bad things and disappointments. There is no lesson to be learned. No loss turning into unexpected gain, grand scheme, sense out of nonsense, order in the chaos, pain bringing you to transcendence, resurrection after the Cross.

If God is impotent, then it would help explain all the pain, disappointment, horror, the stupefying evil done by people, the cruelty of nature. It would explain Christ's saying "Satan is the ruler of this world." And that Christ's peace is not of this world. It would make probable what I suspect: There's a dark destructive force in all of us—not unlike the rapist's. Yet most of us resist evil. Is this learned behavior, societal norms, or is it intuitive knowledge that evil works against us in the end?

After lunch I walk back to my hermitage, past the squirrels swinging from the bird feeder, past the two deer that jump over the fence when they see me. I go to bed, pull a pillow over my head, and although it's the middle of the day, sleep as though I've been knocked out.

Thus I saw God and sought God.
I had God and failed to have God.
And this is and should be
What life is about as I see it.

Julian of Norwich

Every day as I walk on the path that weaves around the property through the woods, I pray my memorized prayers, try to
remember gratefulness, try to hold the belief that God is right
here, right now, try to imagine Christ at my shoulder even
though I don't feel this.

The walk takes only twenty minutes, and after a few times
around each day, I feel like a hamster in a wheel. So I jump the
fence and walk through the neighbor's woods. The forest is dark
and spooky, moss covers everything like witch's hair, vines
snake around trees and dangle to the ground. In the middle of a
small clearing, in a patch of sun, I spot an armadillo tied with
wire, hanging from a tree limb. It doesn't move, and I'm afraid it
was tortured. I try to argue myself out of this. Maybe it was set
out to dry, maybe armadillo skins are used to make cowboy
boots or something.

At dinner when I mention to the nuns that I jumped the
fence onto the neighbor's land, Sister Kathleen, one of the elders,
says, "You could get shot."

I had no idea.

As I walked through those woods I'd felt watched.

I awake in the night, and the bogeyman stares from the
shadow beside the curtain, breathes outside the window, his
hand's at the door.

I'm scared even in daylight. On walks I see a bloated carcass of
a dead dog in the weeds on the side of the road, a rusting rocking

horse on the lawn beside a trailer, a donkey not moving, not even its tail; five black dogs in a yard snarling and barking, trying to jump the fence as I pass; a doll in the grass, its yellow dress in shreds and dirty. I do not want to believe—but I do believe—that the rape opened up a crack through which evil forces are rushing in. I believe the shadowy man in my dreams is an evil spirit, a messenger from the dark. I'm afraid that these beliefs themselves are inviting evil. I know that we see what we choose to see; and that seeing is protective to avoid pain. Sometimes it's in service of the will to live. After the rape, has my will permanently conditioned me toward fear—to see danger and evil everywhere?

I'm sure to the nuns I'm as repulsive as a person covered with oozing boils. I'm in their way. My footsteps, my breathing, my chewing are too loud. I'm the reason they never smile. I forget to catch the screen door before it slams. They think me a glutton because I go for seconds too often and I take too many books from the library to my cabin. I'm the first done with dinner one night and begin to wash dishes. The visiting Dominican sister tells me that we don't waste water by waiting for it to get hot. She pulls from under the sink a gallon jug and runs water into it until the water's hot enough.

"We use this to water the plants," she says, placing the jug on the counter.

Then I observe that this is not always done and feel singled out and picked on. In fact, the nuns are all a little sour, no fun at all. I suspect that because they're of a generation not encouraged to express their feelings, they might not even know they're sick and tired of dealing with retreatants. If I lived here, my body would probably take on a life of its own and start knocking into and breaking things. On a phone call with Estrella, I feel affirmed. I tell her I'm like a bull in a china shop, and she says, "You're too big."

Which I translate as "too much." Kids in the neighborhood

used to say, "Beverly's so crazy she was hatched from a coconut." When we played school, Patty Ryan, the bossy oldest girl who was always the teacher, kicked me out almost as often as she let me in—for laughing too loud, not following directions, asking why.

At home, on her third *pot* of coffee and ever on the verge of a nervous breakdown, my mother screamed, "If I hear that door slam one more time, I'll kill you." My father slapped the dinner table and commanded, "No talking at the table!"

I was a bed wetter. I peed my pants in school; once I peed my pants on the bus ride home. That time I cried so hard I couldn't stop—first from shame about peeing and then from shame about crying. I cried all the time, wailing in the bathroom with the door locked until my father banged on it. "Stop crying before I give you something to cry about."

Am I desperate to believe in God to feel God's love, because I'm too much for anyone else? Am I suffering from God delusion? In fact, honestly, hasn't this whole monastery, retreat house, pilgrimage tour been a delusion? Haven't I lied to myself the whole time, about making God the focus, about finding meaning, when really I just want to live somewhere that is not the scene of the crime; I want to be where I can feel safe.

At Osage negativity went viral.

> Often our trust is not full.
> We are not certain that God hears us,
> Because we consider ourselves worthless and as nothing.
> This is ridiculous and the cause of our weakness.
> I have felt this way myself.
>
> St. Teresa of Avila

I remember that Sister Kay, at Nada, had given me a few pages she'd photocopied from a book about St. Thérèse of

Lisieux, the Little Flower. I've a strong intuition that they'll help me, and one evening I leaf through my papers, then sit in the middle of the floor and read. St. Thérèse's older sister Celine had joined Thérèse's convent and was unhappy with herself for losing her temper, for not being holy, for not being thought much of by the other sisters. St. Thérèse saw that Celine needed to stop constantly striving to be perfect, which Thérèse saw as self-centered and willful—and I see as ego.

Thérèse told her sister to be "willing to bear serenely the trial of being displeasing to yourself, then you will be [for Jesus] a pleasant place of shelter."

I memorize this.

The priest in residence for the month I am here is Father John Vrana, who comes every year on retreat and says mass for the nuns. I have presented him with both of my memoirs and have invited him to dinner. When he suggests driving to Tulsa I am thrilled to be off monastery grounds. Father John is a cancer survivor and so frail I could probably knock him over with a winged-out elbow. He delivers his homilies from a kneeler, referring to notes on pieces of paper the size of an open matchbook, in handwriting as small as sugar ants. Afterward he says, "Now, I'm sure I'm not the only one with opinions here, and I'd sure like to hear what you all have to say." I am too cowed to chime in, but others do, and I'm grateful to Father John for it.

Driving to our dinner, Father John says something I have come to treasure: "Knowing God through the intellect is like someone telling you about their friend, instead of actually meeting their friend. You *know* God; you don't *understand* God."

I have experienced God. I have felt a presence. I have felt loved, and I have loved. I vow to try to keep remembering this.

And also to remember this: If God loves me, who am I not to love myself?

> Before encounter, God is perceived as
> omnipotent power,
> After encounter God is perceived as
> humble love.
>
> Ilia Delio

If I don't tell someone at each place I stay that I have recently been raped, I feel like I'm an impostor. At Desert House of Prayer, I told gentle Sister Jenny, the musician, who listened sympathetically. Then we chatted. She told me she'd been a fifth-grade teacher for years, so I promised to send her my middle-grade book, *Thank You, Lucky Stars*, when it's published, and then she presented me with a lovely poetic translation of the psalms.

At Osage I tell no one until near the end of my stay. I approach Sister Benita after the mass during which we hear the gospel reading in which Peter asks Christ how many times he must forgive, and Christ answers seven times seventy times, but he really means forever.

I tell Sister Benita about the rape and how after I leave Osage I'll be returning to Mexico. I'm not sure when the trial will be, but it's possible it will be soon. And I don't believe I've forgiven the rapist. "It's not like I dwell on him. But I do have nightmares. Sister Benita, how do you forgive, how do you learn to?"

"It's enough that you have the will," she says. "Feelings are feelings, and you can't change them. If we're angry or hurt, it's not who we are. We're like mountains and our feelings are the weather; they come and they go. But you can have the will to forgive. It's the best you can do, and it's a lot. You can ask God to help."

When I was mugged in Mexico and didn't let the thief have my bag, he whirled me in the middle of the street, and while I was imagining the story I'd tell about this, I was also shouting at him in English every obscenity in my extensive book. When he finally did let go because a car turned onto the street, I fell on my ass in the gutter, which was running with water from a rain, and a good thing, because I'd peed my pants. Two college-aged men came to a nearby door and asked if I was okay, and I thought, Fine time to ask.

Only recently did I realize those young men might have come sooner if I'd called "Help!" even once.

I may not feel God's presence, but I know God is here, and I ask for help.

Before the rape, I believed I was a brave person. The fact that I make an appointment to talk with Sister Pascaline gives me hope I still may be. I tell Sister Pascaline how after I leave Osage I will return to my home in Mexico, where I have many friends—a house, lots of things—a life. I tell her I've been off visiting monasteries and retreat centers, that it's been an amazing, deep, and wonderful experience. That I've been thinking I might join a community if I find one that will have me. But I don't know logistically how I would actually manage leaving my old life: my friends, and house, and things.

"Does Mexico bring you closer to God?" Sister Pascaline asks just like that.

"No."

"Then what's the question?"

I wish I could come up with a snappy comeback. Instead my jaw drops.

Back to Mexico, Again

Jesus forgives, and transforms pain,
Which is what we must do.
That's why he says, "Follow me."

Father Richard Rohr

I roll my suitcase through the loftlike living-dining-kitchen area, past the counter where the rapist picked up the knife; past the refrigerator where he stashed a bottle of Bohemia beer; past the *ojo de pollo* on the balcony where he hung his rope ladder; over there is my office where he stole two thousand pesos and change from my wallet.

I'd lived in twenty-four different rentals, nine towns, in four states, and two countries, before I built this house three years ago, the only home that's ever been mine. Everything I own is here: the pillows embroidered with flowers and birds and sweet words, *Te Amo . . . Mi Querida;* my books on shelves where I can see them; a lifetime of paintings reminding me of the friends who painted them, yard sales I found them at, and they all remind me of every house and apartment they've hung in. Cyrano, my beloved cat of seventeen years, is buried in the garden under the St. Francis statue. This is the first house I will never have to leave, and I don't want to admit it, but it may as well be poison ivy.

The Mary icons, twelve of them, their gold halos glowing like fire against the pomegranate wall behind my bed, had looked over my ordeal. They'd been my lifeline to God all the years it took me to paint them. For six years, at least once a week for eight months a year, Mary Jane, a master, and I—along sometimes with others—lit candles, prayed the icon-painting prayer, then sat down and painted in silence to Gregorian chants. Mary Jane mixed egg yolk and water with pigments of ground rocks and gems, then we'd puddle the tempera onto our boards, allowing the pigments to settle where they would, where God willed a shadow. In the first years, Mary Jane was absolutely orthodox about the method. If I applied a line crookedly or too thickly or somehow wrong, I was not allowed to go back and fix it. As we wrote our icons, which are considered a divine dictation, we prayed to God to guide our hands; therefore, what was laid on the board had the hand of God in it and was not to be messed with. Yet one time I'd changed the color of the Virgin's robe so many times, Mary Jane came dangerously close to kicking me out of a group that mainly consisted of Mary Jane and me. These were years of mostly aridity—of searching for but not feeling God's presence. I'm not sure I was trying to discern let alone do God's will, yet I never lost my faith. And the fact that I can't even draw a bunny head yet was able to produce icons of remarkable beauty helped: The icons seemed evidence that God must exist—and involve him- or her- or itself in human affairs.

I haven't seen these icons for longer than six months, not since I left for the monastery tour. But I had been back to San Miguel, a little over a month ago, for a week. Before the rape, I'd committed to give a presentation at a writers' conference, which was scheduled between my stays at Desert House and Osage. A renter was in my house, so I stayed with friends.

This is hard even for me to believe: Making reservations for the trip online, because I so did not want to return to San Miguel, I somehow booked my flight to the neighboring state of Guadalajara instead of to León, Guanajuato—the airport I've flown into so many times my footprints are embedded in the linoleum. It gets worse: I didn't realize my mistake—not when I checked in and was handed my tickets and not when on a layover in Mexico City a gate change was announced, during which the announcer must have said, "Guadalajara." It was as though I weren't in my own body. As I walked to the new gate, I placed one foot in front of the other and the scenery was moving, but I wasn't so sure I was.

When I arrived at the new gate, the world I'd seemed to have been observing through a fuzzy long-distance lens suddenly zoomed in on dozens of short-legged, barrel-bodied Mexican men, every one of them my rapist's double. I took a seat, and the man across the way stared at me, with his legs sprawled. When he smirked, I got dizzy—and dizzier when I noticed I was the only gringo and the only single woman in the waiting area.

I closed my eyes and did some yogic breathing. I tried to be right here, right now in my body with God. I talked myself down. Except for my own fear and the places it can take me, there was nothing to be afraid of here. I thought of the lizard, how ugly I thought it and how beautiful it had become. God is in everyone, I reminded myself, and that's what I wanted to be thinking about right now.

Finally we boarded the plane, and only in lockdown, when there was absolutely nothing I could do about it, did I have ears to hear we were headed to Guadalajara—a city six hours from San Miguel.

I had a meeting at nine the next morning. Since we wouldn't land until ten in the evening, I would have to take a bus, and try to sleep on it.

As soon as I deplaned, I grabbed a cab to the bus station, but the driver told me the last bus for San Miguel had left fifteen minutes ago. I had no choice but to hire a cab and eat the expense. The driver agreed to take me for the equivalent of $170—a bargain since he'd be on the road for at least twelve hours.

When he told me he must first gas up the car and call his wife, I was relieved that he had a wife, which made me realize I was terrified to be alone in a car with a Mexican man, driving in the middle of the night through great distances on a deserted highway. The driver had no front teeth and was in his fifties. The rapist had been in his fifties, too: fifty-eight, to be exact, three years older than I was. His other victims and I had believed him to be much younger, in his thirties, because he'd performed acrobatic maneuvers to get into our houses. He struck on moonless nights, and we couldn't see him if we wanted to, which I, at least, did not. The headline in the paper the day after his capture called him *la rapista de las viajitas*, "the rapist of old ladies." Juan, the special state investigator assigned to the case, told me that in Mexico the only thing worse than raping old ladies is raping children. "When the rapist is convicted," he said, "the jailers will serve him a rope with his dinner to hang himself with."

On the road, the driver asked, "Do you have any children?"

"Yes," I said. "One. He's thirty-eight."

The driver said he had four, all married. And six grandchildren.

I told him I have one grandchild, a boy.

"Do you have a husband?"

Even though in Mexico almost all taxi drivers ask this, I made up a story, "*Sí*. He's waiting for me in San Miguel."

We were weaving our way out of the city on dark, wet streets. It had rained earlier, and in the blackness, the glare of passing

car lights on wet asphalt blinded like camera flashes. Still under
an overpass, I could just make out a mound of flowers and candles, a shrine. *"La Virgen,"* the driver announced.

"Guadalupe!" Tears flooded my eyes at the relief of her name
in the car.

"She appeared here. She appears in my dreams, too."

"¿La verdad? What does she say?"

"Mi hijo. Mi hijo." My son. My son.

"I love her, too." I fought back grateful tears. *"Muchisimo."*

"Ella es mi madre." He looked at me in the rearview.

"Yo tambien." Me, too. I nodded to him. *"Yo tambien."*

Clearly, Mary had sent me an angel.

"¿Como se llama?" I finally asked.

"Juan Carlos."

"Soy Beverly."

"Como Beverly Hills." Almost all taxi drivers say this, too.

Juan Carlos confessed he wasn't exactly sure he knew how to
get to San Miguel, so we read the signs together. Once we made
it onto the highway, he asked if I'd like a blanket, then said, "You
can rest now."

And so I did.

Finally home now and looking at all the Marys on my wall, I
fight an urge to cry. I've missed them, my house, Mexico.

The next day, my maid, Lupe, wakes me when she turns her
key in the street door lock at 7:30. I get up to greet her and she
hugs me, then smiles and nods as she pats both my upper arms
for what seems like a minute.

When I go to the market to buy fruit, Lupe gives a blessing,
"Vaya con Dios," Go with God. She does this whenever I leave
the house, if only for five minutes. St. Bonaventure said a cleaning person can know God much better than a doctor of theology.

And if you could meet Lupe you'd see prayer in action. Lupe once told me she blesses each tortilla she presses.

Lupe comes to my house twice a week and cleans other people's houses four other days in the week, walking miles to town and back to her *ranchito*. She smiles, not wide but constantly, and radiates such peace that one of my friends also hired her, even though she is a little scattered in her chore-doing, is even older than I am, and loses every pair of magnifier glasses I give her, so dishes aren't always spotless. Whenever her other work is done she loves to wash windows. It occurs to me that she's praying as her arm makes circles on the panes, and one day I ask her if this is so. "*Sí, señora.*" She blushes. "*Ruego para usted.*" I pray for you. After I was raped, she had a mass said for me at her church, La Iglesia de San Francisco.

No one knows when the trial will take place, but I have heard it may be soon. This is not something I would mention to Lupe. I love her but don't reveal much to her about my life. Still, I'd stake my reputation as a woman with decent intuition that Lupe's been praying for protection in this house since the rape. She might even be praying that I feel safe here.

But I don't.

In my house even interior doors have locks. I lock every door then walk around every night checking them before bed. When I come home from being out, open the door from the street and see the pineapple palm, my heart thuds as I imagine a man hiding behind it, hiding in a closet, the shower, under a bed. I wake in the middle of the night, almost every night. I sleep with the light on.

And I try to keep up my rule of life—meditation three times a day, reading Lauds and Vespers in the Daily Office, yoga, hikes. After a few weeks, I do pray Lauds and meditate every morning, but skip many afternoons and evenings. Wherever I walk, I pray my memorized prayers. And I pray, "Help me feel your presence, help me see the sacred in every day." I pray, "Give me a sign, show me what I'm to do, where I'm to live. Open the way." I pray, "Help me be of some use. Use me."

I make an appointment with a man I'm told is a world-renowned healer, passing through town. He places his hand on my heart and a few minutes later says, "The saying applies, 'If there's nothing wrong, don't fix it.' Your heart is good, it's strong. You're healed." When I mention that I may become a contemplative at a monastery somewhere he says, "Don't do it. You're not religious, you're spiritual."

"And?" I say impatiently—my equivalent of "Duh."

"Service is the highest calling, maybe you should do something to be of service. What I'm being told is, if you want to reach the next level in this lifetime, you need to help people. I hear there's an orphanage in town. Maybe you could volunteer."

I might have dismissed this healer completely if he hadn't admitted that the only reason he's a healer is because Jesus appeared to him. He'd been a nonbeliever fixing his motorcycle, thinking Jesus nothing more than a historical figure, when Jesus appeared to him and gave him the gift of healing. He had done nothing to deserve it and doesn't know how he does it except to ask for the help of Jesus, who stands by his shoulder.

Self-giving, in other words love, is what Christ did on the Cross. I have almost no instinct in that direction. I am what you call selfish. I have been called selfish. And I wouldn't be surprised if what the healer said is true. Performing some service would stretch my boundaries, help me grow into who God means me to be.

When I spot a sign asking for volunteers to take teenaged girls from the orphanage in the middle of town shopping, I call up the nuns who run the place. It's good timing. I'm asked to come the next day to take a fifteen-year-old named Mariposa. I'm told the girl appeared knocking at the orphanage door the previous evening with nothing but the clothes on her back.

I arrive at 10:00 in the morning, and in the orphanage's old colonial entryway I'm introduced to Mariposa, who's wearing a wool sweater in 80-degree heat that will reach 100 by midday. Her white *tennies* are scuffed and on the little-toe sides torn so that her toes peek out. Mariposa's lush dark hair is in need of a washing; her lips are full and her black eyes large and wide-set like a lion's. Her beauty could make her a target. She is small and unsmiling, her shoulders hunched slightly. I do not want to imagine what—or whom—she is running from.

Mariposa is shy, and on the ride to the San Juan de Dios market stalls on Calle Canal, we talk little, but she does answer a few questions. She tells me she's the oldest of four children, who live with her mother on a *ranchito* in the campo. I have visited *ranchitos* in the campo before and picture a dirt floor, chickens, piglets, goats in the yard, emaciated dogs. A cloth for a door, clothes drying on cacti, and if she's lucky, plants in rusted tin cans nailed to a wall. Signs of poverty for sure but not of unhappiness. I resist but do picture a lecherous boyfriend of her mother, a drooling drunk uncle, a passel of jeering boys.

I offer to buy Mariposa six panties and two bras, but she will accept only two panties and one bra. She will accept two jerseys, one pair of jeans, loafers with copper studs in a g-cleft design, and nothing more.

When I drop Mariposa back at the orphanage, I tell her that if there's anything else she needs, she should call me and we'll shop again. The street is narrow and cars line up behind me as I write my name and phone number on a blank page of my journal, rip it out, and hand it to her. Mariposa takes the paper, nods, and smiles for the first time. She says, "*Gracias,*" pulls her bag of clothes from the car, and runs to the door.

She isn't gone a minute before the road in front of me blurs and I'm choking on sobs. I know that the scenarios of abuse, the lecherous men everywhere she turned, the visual telegraphs my imagination is sending have as much or more to do with me as with Mariposa. It also has to do with our sisterhood with every woman in the world, entire populations, whole generations, raped, oppressed, held captive, abused—as it was in the beginning, is now, and ever shall be. I cannot stand to think these thoughts, I cannot stop these thoughts. I cry till I fall asleep, and in the morning I pick it up without missing a beat. When the tears finally stop, I believe I'm in no condition to help teenaged girls, or probably anyone. And maybe never was.

I remember weeping like this after I'd interviewed for an article a pregnant teenaged girl who'd been kicked out of her house. I remember a writing workshop when a seventh-grade girl stood up and read about her uncle shooting her father in the kitchen, the other kids in class looking at me for my reaction. How my heart hammered in my head, and all I could think to do or say was "Thank you," and talk about how wonderfully detailed, honest, and descriptive the writing was, then I went home and cried.

It's Thomas Merton who helps me not to be too disappointed in myself. I'd heard a tape of a talk he gave to novices when he was the novice master at Gethsemane Trappist monastery in Kentucky. He said we don't have to be generous with gifts we don't have. It's good to ask, What's possible for a person like me?

The answer is as clear now as it has been for most of my life: writing.

In Mexico I finish the middle-grade novel; it's accepted, and

I'm ready for a new project. Before the rape, I'd begun talking with my friend Joe McClain, an opera director, about collaborating on a screenplay, loosely based on a life-changing experience he had when he was fired as director of an opera house he built and founded. Now we talk on long walks down dried riverbeds finding geodes; we traipse through the countryside, getting lost without caring. He cooks for me or I cook for him, and we sit on each other's terraces, brainstorming the whole time, making up a story. Our screenplay has a magical-realism element in which the Virgin of Guadalupe plays a pivotal role. Joe and I divvy up our first scenes and exchange them. He rewrites mine, and I rewrite his. They get better and better. It's fun.

And it's good to see my other friends, too, to hike the botanical preserve, go to yoga class in Bellas Artes, in the cool early morning to walk through its jungly inner courtyard under the building's gracious old porticos. I find a great Zumba class. I resume my Scrabble competition with my friend Lulu, meet with my writers' group of three, watch HBO on Sunday nights with my neighbors Caren and Dave. I begin imagining how I could live my life in San Miguel again.

After I've been in town a few months, the call from the prosecutor arrives: I'm expected to appear at the rapist's trial. Each rape victim will have her own day in court, and mine is scheduled to take place in two weeks.

The trial is held in a room the size of an elementary school classroom, in the new city hall on the outskirts of town. There are three tables, placed in a triangle, and three men chatting behind a grate at the front of the room, where I assume the rapist will appear. I see the prosecutor for the first time since we finalized my deposition almost a year ago. He is clearly overworked and looks worse than he did before. He's tall and hunched; the dark circles under his eyes are puffy, his clothes wrinkled. We shake hands, and he leads me to a table, where he introduces my translator, a young, attractive blond woman I know to be from a prominent San Miguel family. The rapist has hired a defense attorney, dapper with a feathered haircut, wearing a smart suit at the table next to ours.

I ask the translator, "Where's the rapist?" and she shushes me, whispering, "He's there. Behind the grate. The one in the middle."

Never in a million years would I have chosen that man in a lineup. He looks like somebody's father. He wears glasses that make him appear intellectual, a cardigan sweater with leather patches on the elbows, and a short beard. The rapist looks comfortable.

There can be no question it's him; his DNA was a match in all five rapes.

When I first heard I'd be coming to trial, I prayed for help getting through the ordeal, for healing and closure. But my prayers have changed. I've been praying that God make something good come of the rape, and of this trial. The first line of the song of the St. Francis prayer has been playing in my mind for two weeks, as it does right now, "Make me a channel of your peace."

"Use me," I pray.

In Mexico the accused has the right to face the accuser, and the Mexicans seem to have taken the dictum literally. The rapist remains behind the grate, so throughout the trial we face each other. The judge, a woman, soon enters and sits at a desk nearer the rapist and between us. She faces sideways, in profile like a priest in a confessional, with the rapist on one side, me on the other.

The rapist doesn't look at me.

I stare at him. There seems a haughtiness, something prideful and condescending in his comfortable stance, and he reminds me of the men at a Donofrio family gathering I attended in New Haven years ago. The women sat at large round tables in a banquet room while the men sat at small tables in the dark bar beside it. My sister and I wanted a drink and walked into the bar to order one. We liked it in there, so we took a seat. All eyes were on us, so we smiled at the room in general. Nobody smiled back, or looked at us again. They conveyed that we were being actively ignored, that we were not only not welcomed, we were below their attention, and convicted of the worst sin: disrespect of their sovereignty to inhabit a bar without being disturbed by such as us. In some translations "fear" in the Bible is translated as respect. Show respect, or God may throw another flood at you.

My latest and greatest therapist, Valerie, half English by descent but all Mexican by nationality, believed I moved to Mexico to re-create the culture of my childhood. And she may be right.

In the courtroom, I do not drop my stare for more than a few seconds. If he finally decided to look at me we could end up in a staring match. Maybe I'm doing what they tell you *not* to do when confronted by an aggressive dog.

My deposition is read first, and when I'm asked if I have anything to add, I say, "No. It's all there."

"Do you recognize the man?" the judge asks.

"Yes," I lie. "He's there."

"But you said he was younger in your statement," she reminds me.

"Yes. It was dark. I couldn't see. But he was this man's size." This is the truth. "His height and his weight. And the FBI matched his DNA."

The rapist's lawyer jumps to his feet, objecting with much

force. "What does the FBI have to do with this? Is it because she believes the FBI that she believes this man raped her?"

"What do you know about the FBI report?" the judge asks me.

Obviously, I've made an error. I know well the Mexican saying, "*Pobre* Mexico, so close to the United States, so far from God." I know that Mexicans, especially educated Mexicans, feel their country is like a mouse pushed into a corner by a herd of elephants—rude farting elephants that never watch where they're stomping. And the FBI would be seen as an elephant rider.

I'm well practiced at interrogative repositioning. My father was a detective, suspicion his middle name, and I was in trouble a lot. I am absolutely unflustered when I say, "The special investigator assigned to this case told me about the FBI report. I believe the strongest evidence that this man is the rapist is that since his capture, not a single woman has been raped."

The judge nods, and if I read the look on her face correctly, she thinks I've just made a good point about the more-than-yearlong absence of rapes in the town—which amazingly, she seems not to have thought of herself.

She tells me that because I didn't fight, it appears I may have consented to sexual relations.

I tell her I didn't fight because I'd heard the stories of the other women. I'd heard that the first two who'd fought had been beaten up and raped anyway. The next two had not fought and had not been beaten up. I didn't fight, because I knew he would win and I didn't want to be beaten up as well as raped. "He had a knife," I finally remember to say, and when I say it it's with the intonation of You have got to be kidding me.

The judge seems satisfied.

While the rapist's deposition is read, the rapist crosses his arms against his chest and lifts his chin. In his deposition he confessed he'd have a few beers, then break into gringo women's houses to steal a few trinkets and cause a "little mischief." At the conclusion of his deposition, when he, too, is given the opportunity to speak, he runs with it, talking for what feels like three hours but is probably one. He's a politician on the stump, a working-class hero on a soapbox. He's the downtrodden voice of the people. He couldn't get work in Mexico so he was forced to live in the United States for twenty-five years. He was put in jail and treated like a dirty dog. Gringos outside of jail treated him like a dirty Mexican dog, too. Women used him for sex. Now he's too old for anyone to hire. What's he supposed to do? How's he supposed to eat? "These gringo women are ruining the good name of my grandparents."

The rapist believes he's the victim.

In this he is not so different from my ex-husband, the junkie, whom I tracked down to sign a release for the movie version of *Riding*. I found him in a rooming house in Secaucus, New Jersey, feeling sorry for himself. After being led to the second floor by a guy who'd been drinking from a paper bag, I heard my ex-husband ranting behind his door, "I get no respect. I'm fucking forty fucking years old, and I get no fucking respect." When he opened the door to my knock, he said, "Do I know you?" followed shortly by, "Shit, it's my ex-wife. You look better than when I went out with you. You wrote a book. I saw that book. I didn't read it. I wanted to see what you look like now. You made a lot of money. You should give me some."

He had stolen money from his son's piggy bank. He'd cashed in his son's savings bonds; he never paid a cent of alimony or child support. And he never even asked how his son is. It was a blessing that he was out of our lives, it's true, but it enraged me that he cared nothing for his child, for our son, for Jason, my boy, who deserved better. And the fact that he thought I owed him something made me want to commit murder.

When the rapist finally finishes his own rant, I ask the judge if I can say something.

"On the record?" she asks.

"No. I don't care. I just want to say something to him." She nods permission, and I say, "I came from a poor family, too. I wanted to be a writer, I wanted an education, but there was no money for college. Like you, I used to be angry about what I didn't have and what I couldn't do and how unfair life is. But only when I started taking responsibility for myself did life get good, and was I finally happy. You need to take responsibility. You need to apologize for what you did—"

"I'm not apologizing to you," he snarls.

"You don't have to apologize to me, you have to apologize to God." His apology would have been very nice, indeed. But more than anything I want good to come of the rape, and I suspect that telling him to apologize to God is a suggestion he might actually one day be able to hear. And an apology to God is more important. Evil is never recognized as evil by those who do it; if he's to have a chance, he must acknowledge he did wrong.

The rapist says something in reply, and the judge orders it not be translated.

"I want to hear what he said," I insist.

The judge nods to my translator, who says, "He said, 'God bless you.'"

The judge may have thought he was being sarcastic, or that he had no right to be giving me a blessing from God, but I choose to accept the blessing. "Thank you," I say to the rapist, who still will not look at me.

The trial is over, and the translator shakes her head as she pats my hand. "You're too good," she says, and I do not have the feeling she means it as a compliment.

Afterward I pray for the rapist a few times, but it doesn't feel sincere.

I plan to work on it.

> "He abused me, he beat me, he defeated me, he robbed
> me"—In those who harbor such thoughts hatred
> will never cease.
> "He abused me, he beat me, he defeated me, he robbed
> me"—In those who do not harbor such thoughts
> hatred will cease.
> "For hatred does not cease by hatred at anytime; hatred
> ceases by love—this is an old rule.
>
> The Dhammapada or "Path of Virtue"

September is my favorite month. The weather is beautiful no matter where in the world you are, and in San Miguel pink cosmos blanket the countryside like God took a paintbrush to it. I was born in September, and as my birthday approaches, I spark with such longing for prayer in chapel, for silence so profound it's as the psalmist said, "Deep calls on deep"; that I know: I must be away and still, at a monastery. I know there are people who can experience God anywhere, but I'm not strong, or practiced, enough, and may never be. I'm hoping to one day know that a monastery is where I belong—where God wants me—for the rest of my life. I want to contemplate eternity and from that far reach, maybe I'll rebuild the home inside that was broken into. I long for the feeling of presence, the feeling of being loved. I know what I must do with such certainty; God might as well have hired a plane to paint a message in the sky: "Get thee to a monastery."

Nada is a retreat center and hermitage, but it's a monastery to me. And even though Sister Kay said they weren't considering new people, Nada is calling. Nada in the shadow of a mountain, Nada in the fierce desert, Nada with a chapel open twenty-four hours a day with its Jesus lifting off his cross. At Nada instead of a distraction at my fingertips, the Internet is a walk away in the main building's library, where ten thousand books await a reading. At Nada there is no TV, a tiny hermitage with everything I need, other people living the same life; a sky whose enormousness is so ever-present, I've heard of people being frightened by the wide-openness.

I pray in faith, "Your will, not mine," I pray, "Open the way," but my faith isn't strong enough, so I worry: Even if they weren't in flux, what community in their right minds would accept an aging woman with family she must visit, and more discouragingly, no pension to offer? But perhaps if I could work a few hours each week helping to support the place and pay them some money, sort of as rent, then I would not only be allowed to write for the amount of time I'd need each day, but I wouldn't be perceived as a liability.

I am almost out of money, but I will soon receive the last of three payments for the middle-grade book, *Thank You, Lucky Stars*. I have an invitation to write about the rape for *O* magazine, and a lecture to deliver in a few months at a college in Connecticut. Less commissions, this will total about $12,000 for the year. Not much, considering I would also have to pay for at least two flights but preferably three back east from Colorado to fulfill my commitment to be involved with Zach and my aged parents. When I factor in what I might make after expenses by renting my house, I figure I will have $16,000 in income for the year, which should be exactly enough.

I call Nada and suggest that I come for six months on a trial basis. I will pay $600 a month and buy my own food. I will work with the community some but will need enough time to be able to write.

And they welcome me.

MONK

The monastery is the place we do battle
to bring the reign of God into
our lives and our world.

The Rule of St. Benedict

At Nada

Pray as though everything depended on God,
Work as though everything depended on you.

St. Augustine

They say that when you're moving in the right direction, doors fly open and God strews flowers in your path. But not always. Sometimes faith is required—which may be the same as saying you have to work for the grace.

When I left Santa Monica for Mexico in 1999, I was on fire with my new love for the Virgin Mary and wanted to live in a country that called her its mother. That first day on my way through the Mojave Desert, four hours from Santa Monica, I stopped to get gas, placed my bag on the car trunk, and a thief ran off with it. I was afraid God was telling me not to leave and had just smacked me back to where I'd started from. Especially once I realized that not only was my checkbook gone, along with four hundred one-dollar bills to present in wads for bribing, but also my passport and car registration, without which I would not be allowed to cross the border. Luckily I'd held my wallet in my hand and still possessed my driver's license and credit card. I'd seen no one take my bag, but when I told the gas station attendant what had happened, he said he'd heard someone peel out, and we assumed it was the thief. I called the police to report it and waited inside the air-conditioned Texaco station. It was a blistering 114 degrees, and when I returned to the car, I found my angel-winged begonia, which I'd wedged between two boxes in the backseat—the beloved plant I'd lugged with me for ten years, the only one I planned to smuggle into Mexico—dead, its leaves black and limp as reposed bat wings.

That was it. I turned around and headed back to LA, where because my leaving had been so sad for both of us, I was sure Renee, my housemate, would welcome me back. There, I'd file for my documents and try for Mexico again—or not. Along the way, I stopped to buy water at a convenience store and spilled my sad story to the friendly young woman at the register.

"What's wrong with people?" she said. "See them holes up there?" High up on the window were four bullet holes. "A guy paid for beer with pennies, and when the night manager asked him to count 'em out, he shot the window."

The gun shooter and my thief conflated into one no-good, low-down, bad-news jerk; and I got mad. Was I going to be bullied by a cowardly little thief into abandoning my dreams? I pointed my car to Mexico again, trying not to worry about not heeding the signs, and remembering how when I went on pilgrimage to Medjugorje the pilgrims had told stories about a force trying to prevent their going; there'd been illnesses, loss of money, even a death.

I made phone calls, sent away for supporting documents, I photocopied, faxed, filed, shelled out five hundred dollars, then ten days later, my new passport and car registration caught up with me on the Mexican border, where I'd been waiting for them. I was now broke, all the more reason to buy myself a treat. I'd cross the next day into Mexico, and for a celebratory reward I decided to go to the mall and buy some new music. For ten years I'd been looking for what I thought to be a Neville Brothers tape, a copy of which a friend I'd met on a vacation in Mexico had sent me. The tape ended with *"Ave Maria,"* which cut off right after the luscious musical introduction, with Aaron singing "AAAAAAAV—" This time, at a Sam Goody's, I noticed that beside the Neville Brothers section was a section called Aaron Neville, and finally, ten years after my search had begun, on the border with Mexico, I found her. I hugged that CD to my chest; finding something I'd always missed but never lost surely had to be a sign.

The guard at the border asked me to open my trunk. A painting of the Virgin Mary was on top of everything. I told him I was writing a book about La Virgen. He told me he was interested in esoteric mysticism and waved me right through. I was waved through every checkpoint. There was no traffic; the roads were smooth.

After four hours, I'd played all the CDs, except for Aaron Neville, which I'd saved for last. Its turn came at the foot of the Sierra Madres. I climbed up and up. I wound around. I passed chugging, exhaust-spewing trucks—and then I was alone on the road up above the clouds. There were century plants in bloom, maguey and cacti, and green all around. As I crested the top of the mountain I could see to the horizon in every direction. An eagle rode on the wind by my window, two baby pigs tripped out from a bush, and I heard the beginning strains followed by a heartbreakingly wavery *Aaaaave Mariiiiaaaa gracia plena . . .*

Tears poured down my face. In Mexico there's a saying, *con fe se tiene todo,* with faith you have everything. I wanted to believe this. It was the time of my life to live as though I did.

And I had tried.

I'd like to report that something resembling that miraculous trip happened when I arrived at Nada in October 2007. But my arrival was so uneventful, I do not remember it.

And I don't take this as a sign.

> In returning to me and resting in me
> You shall be saved;
> In quietness and truth shall be your strength.
>
> Isaiah

It's Saturday night, 7 p.m., 10 below zero, and almost Thanksgiving; the stars crackle so thick and bright, the glittered sky is so enormous, my heart leaps like a deer bounding through the prairie. It's so dark, I can't see two feet in front of me down the curvy dirt road to Compline. So I'm shining my flashlight angled down, to not diminish the huge wild blackness, saying for the hundredth time since I arrived with two suitcases over a month ago, "Thank you, God. Thank you, God. Thank you, God."

As I walk in the dark I'm not afraid of the mountain lion a retreatant spotted sleeping in a tree near my hermitage; or the mountain lion Kay spotted playing in the middle of a dirt road; I'm not afraid of the black bear I saw trundling over a neighbor's fence; I'm not afraid of the coyotes screaming hysterically at cornered prey. They're all part of the wildness here, like the lightning that ricochets off Mount Carmel; like a double rainbow; a fire-red, cloud-tumbled sky rolling toward the San Juans at sunset; wind devils; tumbleweed; a fox tail disappearing in a stand of pinions; thunder shaking the building. Or a voice calling in the wilderness, "Be still and know that I am God."

My hermitage, Thérèse, is not only more than twice the size of my first hermitage, Gandhi, but also more functional; I've desk enough to write three books at the same time, I've file drawers enough to store all the books' research and drafts, shelves enough to read a book a week for a few years and keep them all. I've a comfy rocker with a gliding foot stool, a window seat, kitchen sink, two burners built in; counters would be nice, but I'm not complaining; I've a bathtub, and a closet so wide there's empty space. If I designed a 300-square-foot house, I'd design this one. I cannot see another building, and the sun sets outside my kitchen window.

It's named after St. Thérèse of Lisieux, the Little Flower, who died of TB at twenty-four, in excruciating pain, having lost her lifelong comfort of God's presence, but not the faith that God was still there. (This is a deathbed phenomenon experienced by many saints—and I wonder if it's what Christ experienced in the Garden of Gethsemane.) The picture on the wall of my bedroom must have been taken not long before St. Thérèse took to bed. There are puffy circles under tired, intelligent eyes that seem to take you in rather than look at you. The saint is famous for her "Little Way": loving God by doing little favors, treating others with unending kindness, loving God through her small actions and little chores, loving God by *being* the love of God. I still repeat to myself her sage words to her sister Celine: be "willing to bear serenely the burden of being displeasing to yourself." Thérèse promised that when she died she'd be up in heaven sending down blessings. Her picture looking down at me as I sleep does make me feel blessed. But not safer.

My roof is a free-for-all at night like Gandhi's had been, and when I awake in the middle of the night, the darkness in the hermitage does not feel filled with wonder; the darkness is small and contained, hot and in lockdown, and like freedom from it will require a prison break. I have experienced the same repeat nightmare everywhere I have slept, so I must conclude it's a fixture inside of me. Yet, since the rape, I have been most afraid during my first visit at Nada and now again while living here.

Nada was also where I first experienced Jesus' presence at my shoulder, and shortly after I arrive this time, I sense him again.

Whenever I think to look for him, there he is. But strangely I don't remember him the moment I awake frightened. It takes a while.

I've read that it takes seven years to heal from a trauma and that seven years is how long it takes a body to make every cell new. I've also read that every seven years a life change occurs. And when I look at my life, it seems true: 21, arrest for possession of marijuana and put on probation; 28, graduation from college and move to NYC; 35, my work published for the first time; 42—I can't think of anything besides my first visit to LA, for six weeks to write a TV show; 49, move to San Miguel; 56, I am raped and head off for the monastery tour.

I've heard of rock musicians who replace every drop of their own blood with the blood of strangers to kick drug addictions. If there were cell-replacement transfusions, as well, and if I were rich, I might sign up for both.

At least for now, I'm able to avoid thinking how the world God designed buzzes with evil like wasps around an endangered nest. Every day when I pray the Liturgy of the Hours and read the psalms that deal with cruelty and war, I translate them as poems about interior battles.

I do not consider blaming God for all the suffering and evil in this world a road to healing, but I do consider talking about my rape a boulevard. So, that's what I do at more than a few Sunday brunches. One of the monks or I will have arisen at dawn—or before—to prepare the meal, then after mass, the five monks—Kay, Suzy, Connie, Thomas, Eric—and I will sit down with however many retreatants are in residence that week. Because I've arrived in off-season, that means there usually will be in total anywhere from eight to a dozen people at table—in season there can be as many as eighteen. We say grace, briefly introduce ourselves, then hold one conversation, during which I've been known to squeeze in the rape. A retreatant might say, "I left the church after I married twenty years ago, and I still don't go to mass. But there's something about the intimacy of your chapel. Maybe it's the wilderness, the silence. I don't know. Something. I'm asking a lot of questions."

And I will say, "I've been working on questions myself. I was raped a year and a half ago, and instead of asking, 'Why me,' I'm trying to focus on the more important question, 'What am I going to do now that it's happened; what do I have to learn?' " Then I'll tell that he was a serial rapist . . . I prayed *Hail Marys* and chased him out . . . the rape itself lasted only two minutes . . . I always try to include the last to diminish their seeing me as too much of a victim.

I've never asked the monks what they thought of my repeat rape confessions that first year. I didn't get to know Thomas and Kay well enough. After a meeting the monks held in January, Kay would leave for a secular life, and Thomas would be required at the hermitage in Ireland. But I can imagine Suzy saying, "It was what you needed. It was fine. Fine. It was real." Connie would nod and shrug, "You gotta do what you gotta do." And Eric would nod, too, but underneath he'd be resisting presenting a deadpan face to joke, "You were raped?"

During vespers one time, it was my turn to choose a reading, which I love to do, because then I get to read it and exercise my true vocation—according to an aptitude test I took when I was twenty-two—of dramatic reader. It was just the four of us in chapel. I stood at the lectern and, assuming the persona of God, read dramatically the opening question: "Who am I?"

Eric responded, "Bev?"

The monks and I make one another laugh. They ask about my family and I about theirs. They sit through *Saturday Night Fever* when one birthday, for their cultural enrichment, I make them. They eat my pasta even though they don't want to get fat.

And they are patient, oh, so patient. They've all been working at treating the other person as Christ for more than twenty years, some of them almost thirty. I do not feel like they talk about me behind my back. I must annoy them sometimes, but they are good at not showing it.

Supposedly, by being obedient to the life—the schedule of services, the work prescribed, the committed hours of prayer—monks get to experience what it's like to say, "Your will, not mine," to ignore the demands of their own egos, and ideally give the ego less power to run the show. Not having so many choices, not giving in to the needs of our egos to do what we want, when and how we please, is said to bring peace. It's sort of a rehearsal for the larger letting go, the total surrender, the absolute Yes to God, your will, not mine, that saints and enlightened beings make.

Although my schedule of work and communal and solitary prayer is not so rigorous as it would be if I were a Benedictine or a Trappist or even a full-time working member of this hermitage—even though there is still plenty of "I want" and "I need to do" at play in my life, and even though so many nights are troubled—I feel more peace here than I ever knew I could. I'm woven into the rhythm of mass at noon on Wednesdays, Thursdays, Fridays, and at nine on Sundays; vespers on Wednesdays and Thursdays; Lauds, followed by chores, on Saturday mornings; and Compline on Saturday evenings. The amount of communal and private prayer is a perfect balance for me. As are the time of communal work and the many hours left for my writing.

These are my duties: As I mentioned, I take my turn cooking Sunday brunches, which follow Sunday masses. Once a week I'm housemaster, which means I'm stationed at the main house to answer the phone, launder linens, greet anyone who might stop by, make a run into our little town of Crestone for the mail and to pick up anything that's needed from Curt's, the local store.

Every few weeks I make the town trip, which means spending the day running errands in Alamosa, the larger town an hour south through the San Luis Valley. There, I gas up the van and wash its windows. Often a post office stop is necessary to pick up mailing bins not available at our local office; books must be returned to the library, a prescription picked up, a gadget purchased from the hardware store, health cat food bought from the vet (two huge, red brother cats, Tigger and Hobbs, live in Cup and Sword, the house reserved for the monks' use). And to keep the refrigerator stocked and the cupboards filled—ten heads of broccoli, twenty pounds of carrots, three dozen apples, a dozen cans of tomato soup, four jars of Skippy peanut butter, ten pounds of flour, et cetera—always there's shopping at Safeway, Walmart, and the food co-op.

Have I mentioned I have ADD? My first town trip took me *twelve* hours; on a subsequent town trip I'm so rattled trying to remember when to use a check and when to use the debit card, to write down every penny spent and for what, where I put the shopping list and in what sequence to do things, smoke comes out my ears; and in the Safeway parking lot, with a van jammed full, I lock the keys in the car while it's still running.

Then I consider not telling anyone, so the monks—whom I've taken to calling "the monkles"—won't know what they've gotten themselves into by inviting me into their hermitage and trusting me with chores.

But because I'm trying to be genuine, to hide nothing, I feel it's only fair they know who I am and what they're getting.

I return after Vespers, and Suzy is alone in Agape. As we lug thirty bags of groceries into the kitchen, I confess that I locked the keys in the running car and had to call a locksmith. She laughs, then says, "Oh, poor baby, welcome to the club. Listen, half the time I'm lucky I remember my name."

God may be reached
And held close by means of love,
But by means of thought never.

The Cloud of Unknowing

This Saturday night, when I reach the chapel, I take off my shoes in the vestibule but it'll be cold in the chapel, so I keep on my coat and hat and gloves. I step inside, press a palm to my heart, and look up at Jesus, who as always seems about to bust loose and fly straight off his cross. I say, "Jesus, sweetheart, hi, it's so good to see you, darling, bunny love, pumpkin pie," names I call my grandson and called my beloved, now deceased cat Cyrano for seventeen years. It is not very reverent, but I'm more interested in a personal relationship than I am in fear and awe and trembling, although I suppose there's some of that, too. Lately, every time I enter the chapel and look at Jesus—his eyes looking up so expectantly, his body straining closer to when the suffering will end—he feels so human and hopeful, so dear and sweet and cuddly, I have to gush. I do not do this aloud.

I bow, take a seat in the second row, and try to still my mind as I await Benediction, my favorite service. When Connie and Kay, Suzy, Thomas, and Eric arrive, two will sit on each bench angling out from the altar—when Kay and Thomas are gone, Connie will sit on one side and Eric on the other. Suzy takes a chair like I do, because her back does not do well on wooden benches.

We will sing in Latin, candles will be lit, and bells will ring as the host is placed inside the sunburst monstrance, which will then be incensed with a swinging thurible. (One day the incensing will be my job.) We'll sing "Salve Regina" and end with a profound bow.

Waiting, I sit cross-legged in the chair and close my eyes, feeling as content as a child cozy in a stroller, carried along, heading someplace that remains a mystery till I get there with no effort of my own.

In Exodus, up on Mount Horeb, God told Moses to go tell the people that every seven years they are to take a sabbatical, let their fields lay fallow, and perform not one lick of work. They were meant to relax and play, refuel, reflect, commune with God, be a still cup to receive divine love, spirit, knowing. A sabbatical marks the space between the end of one time and the beginning of another, a pause between breaths, a renewal and an education.

I do not believe that my time at Nada is a sabbatical. After my first half year, if the monks will have me, I believe I'll make my life here.

Going to the Chapel

Juniper

It's my first Christmas at Nada and the first of my life I'll celebrate with people who believe as the Advent prayer in my hymnal says, "A savior was born of Mary, and a light dawned on us in radiant beauty." We've been anticipating Christmas all through Advent but won't have strung lights, arranged a crèche, hung a single wreath until Christmas Eve.

Christmas Eve day, Eric and Thomas will go up on the mountain to cut down a tree for Agape, and Suzy, Connie, Kay, and I will decorate the chapel to prepare for the crowd expected at midnight mass. Connie, Suzy, and Kay gathered garbage bags full of evergreen branches yesterday, but more are needed to create a veritable forest against the back chapel walls and at the base of the altar. Having procrastinated gathering my share, I will go this morning.

When I awake there's a foot of snow on the ground, and it's still snowing. By the time I've prayed and meditated and bundled up, the snow is coming down hard. There are no cars on the unplowed roads as I navigate our Chevy Blazer down to Willow Creek, park off the road, grab a few garbage bags, some loppers and clippers, and walk into the trees. The snow is almost to my knees, the air so silent and still, I feel outside of time, like there's only one place, and it's right here, in this moment.

As all around me snow falls and falls, I weave through a thicket of evergreens, looking for the junipers with the most abundant clusters of dark-blue berries. Each time I find one, I gaze up at its bluish green, pine-smelling magnificence and thank God from the bottom of my heart for its being, for the existence of junipers. Each time I cut a branch, I thank the juniper for giving such a gift, for decorating our chapel, for helping to celebrate Christ's birthday, for making Christmas so Christmas.

Greening

Too soon after Christmas the monks from Ireland are arriving for a long-planned-for community meeting, during which they are to discuss plans for the future. On the agenda is talk about whether or not to accept lay and/or temporary members and what those arrangements would look like. This discussion will directly impact me, so I had been informed, even before I arrived, that in January I would have to leave.

The timing couldn't be worse, and it couldn't be better. I'm so neatly knitted into the rhythm of communal prayer that I know when the bell calling us to chapel is going to ring, without looking at a clock. Meditating with the others in chapel feels like coming home out of the rain. All the hours contemplating Jesus on his cross—how we worship a God who's been spat at and beaten and stripped of his clothes, a God whose friends have deserted him, a God who presents himself as the last thing anyone wants to be—is accessing something in me I can't put a finger on yet, and it's hard to leave.

On the other hand, the timing couldn't be better, because I can celebrate a belated Christmas with my family, and I can attend a low-residency MFA program at Wilkes University, in Wilkes-Barre, Pennsylvania, to which I've been invited. My friend Kaylie Jones, a founding faculty member, has recommended me, and if I like the program, and the faculty and administration like me, then a job as instructor could be the answer to how I will continue to afford to live at Nada. I'd mentor each student via the Internet through the writing of a novel or memoir, and I will have to be on campus for only one week in January and one in June—trips that could dovetail with visits to my family in Brooklyn and Connecticut. I will be paid per student, and the money isn't much, but if I take on at least three students a semester, it, along with the $4,000 a year I can get, after mortgage and other expenses, for renting my house, and a freelance magazine article here and there, will be enough to cover expenses every year.

I visit my parents for almost a week and escape their blaring TV by seeing friends and visiting the library. My mother's emphysema has gotten so bad that she barely leaves the sofa, and my father has heroically risen to the occasion and become the grocery shopper, housekeeper, and cook. Sometimes my mother sits at the table and instructs, and sometimes she'll cut vegetables. But more often my father does it all. This has been going on for a while, so my father requires less and less instructing now. He watches cooking shows on TV, has collected some nice pots and pans, and has become a good cook. A maid comes once a week for a few hours to do the major cleaning, but not the washing of the kitchen floor. My father's afraid she'll use too much water, causing the linoleum to peel up, so he does the job himself. To give him a break, I do laundry, scour sinks and the tub, wipe down the blinds, and cook some of their basic dinners: beef

stew, linguine with clam sauce, ham and cabbage boiled with po-
tatoes and carrots. I like to cook, and this could be fun if it
weren't for my father's hovering and questioning my every
pinch of salt. Not in a manner that suggests he's trying to learn,
but in a manner that suggests he suspects I don't know what I'm
doing.

It's not so different at my son's house. Jase is the stay-at-home
dad, and like his grandfather, he does the grocery shopping and
cooking. But he allows the maid to wash all floors and is happy
to hand over the cooking reins as often as I'd like to take them.
When his wife, Jessica, gets home from her job at an investment
bank, we enjoy a meal in the dining room, trying to coax Zachary to eat at least something. During the days, I take Zach for
walks and playtime at one of several parks we can walk to from
his house.

One weekend I borrow Jase's car and take Zach to my friend
Nancy's. She lives on the bay in Cutchogue on the North Fork of
Long Island, where Zach and I had come when he was a year old,
and I thought I'd drop dead from exhaustion. He's two and a half
now and no calmer, but he doesn't need to be held as much and is
entertained by Nancy's three dogs, with whom he runs all around
the large hilly yard. Since neither Jason nor Jessica believes in
God and Zach receives virtually no exposure, I make a point of
saying things like, "Thank you, God, for making dogs who like to
lick Zachary's face. Thank you, God, for my darling *niñeto* sweet
pumpkin pie love-of-my-life grandson. I love him So Much."

It rains on Saturday, so we all go to the Aquarium in River-
head. It's Zach's first time, and he runs from here to there,
presses his face against the glass of the tanks, beside himself
with excitement, practically trembling as he says, "Fish!" We
wander downstairs, and in a large tank a seal swims right up to
the glass then at the last second does a back flip and swims away

out of sight. We wait, and it comes back and does the same thing with a grin on its face. This time, the moment the seal disappears, Zach shouts, "Here he comes, here he comes," over and over until the seal shows up again, and then he laughs and claps. This must happen twenty times over. By which time a crowd of little kids has gathered, some of them in strollers, all of them shouting, "Here he comes, here he comes."

Upstairs we discover that the seal was putting on a show above the water and, in between tricks, swam down to give us a thrill, which makes me think that God can be to me like the seal is to Zach. Not that God's doing tricks or is in only two places at once, but everywhere, every second, all the time. And all we have to do is be like Zach, with total faith, calling out, "Here he comes, here he comes." Or better yet, "Here he is."

At the Wilkes residency, I meet the faculty, most of whom seem so familiar I could have known them for decades already. I think at the time, Ah, writers, my birds of a feather. Except I don't laugh nearly as much as others do and suspect that I might once have but am now incapable. I tell everyone I'm a self-avowed nun, and when I show up at a cocktail party with a gorgeous necklace—a long string of semiprecious stones arranged in clusters—Nancy McKinley, who is as Irish Catholic as St. Patrick, says, "You sure don't dress like a nun," to which I respond in all sincerity, "I'm not wearing lipstick."

During the week, I talk to many students, sit on a nonfiction panel, and give a ten-minute reading along with the other faculty members, who are poets and novelists and nonfiction writers. The faculty is so large that the readings must be divided into two evenings, one in a banquet-sized room in the student union and the other at Barnes and Noble. I choose short pieces from both *Riding* and *Looking for Mary*—to introduce my work—and read them in the banquet-sized room.

I am pleased when I'm asked to join the faculty, and at the next residency, in June, I decide to read the scene of the rape, a version of which I have written. This time I'm slated to read at Barnes and Noble, where the lectern is positioned in front of the storefront window, which opens onto the town square. Awaiting our turns, the poet Christine Galineau says, "Nothing like giving the whole town a view of our asses."

As I read about the night of the rape, in a packed store, in front of faculty I hope will become friends, students who might become my mentees, and a hundred or so total strangers, I feel fierce and commanding. "This," I am saying without actually saying the words, "you must know about me." In my reading there is no humor, no distance, just the facts, thank you very much, ma'am. My reading could be a course on how not to write memoir, or on mistaking undigested experience as anything more than raw material. I do not think any of this at the time. In fact, I think God and I have processed what happened to me just fine. I am darkly serious; I am all about letting everyone know that this woman is writing about the only important subject worth tackling: God.

I might have reminded myself about the time, for a fundraiser, I showed a documentary about the twentieth anniversary of Eve Ensler's *Vagina Monologues*. At the end of the documentary, Eve Ensler and a group of famous actors—all rape victims—bow on a New York stage after giving a performance of the play. Eve Ensler asks anyone in the audience who's been raped to please stand. More than half the audience did, and in the smaller theater audience in San Miguel, two women stood up, too, arms around each other, crying. I thought, There but for the grace of God . . . ; I thought, Poor women; I'm not so sure I'd stand up and let everyone know.

Since that viewing, as you know, I was raped. As you also

know, I have talked to plenty of people about it. But always in conversation and never in front of more than one hundred strangers.

After the reading, I approach Bonnie Culver, a playwright and the program's director, and tell her, "I don't ever, ever want to read at Barnes and Noble ever again." I actually believe the reason I give: "I can't stand to have my fat ass on display for the whole world to see."

Perhaps being in denial about how upset about the rape I really am is not so dissimilar to being in shock; otherwise I might have cried in front of everyone, like I do six months later in a packed chapel on the feast day of St. John of the Cross, July 16. This is the day the monks renew their vows of poverty, obedience, and chastity. Our congregation, which worships with us on Sundays, is here, and so are dozens I've never seen before. A few Sufis wear turbans, there are a few saris, and members of a Hindu group are dressed all in white. Crestone is a Mecca for spiritual centers—at last count there were twenty—and since the taking of vows is considered a spiritual act to be honored, people have come to celebrate with us. Extra chairs had to be brought in, and a few sit on the steps that lead to the pit in front of the altar.

I've been sitting on a wooden bench down there, next to Connie, who no longer wears her monk outfit, nor does Suzy, sitting across from us next to Eric on the other bench. At the meeting in January, the community voted to open its doors to lay and temporary members, and it also agreed to permit current religious members to change their status to permanent lay members if they chose to. This is what Connie and Suzy have elected to do.

I'm not sure *elected* is the word I'd choose for my decision to make temporary vows; it was too of the moment and organic for that and had happened only two Fridays ago. That morning I awoke sliding my cheek on a dusting of sand on my pillow. It was hot, and I'd left the window next to my bed open, and because it's almost level with the ground, a bucketful of sand had blown in. I procrastinate doing housework as long as I possibly can, but the sand couldn't be ignored and it was time to bite the bullet. I remembered Brother Lawrence and his advice to practice the presence of God. So I stripped the bed, saying, "God, I dedicate this to you." Bringing God into the picture makes me pay closer attention, and paying closer attention can make things more interesting. I felt the breeze of the sheet as it billowed down; I made large arching sweeps with my arms as I smoothed the sheets then snapped them as I tucked them in. I was mesmerized by the play of sunlight on the suds as I rinsed them off my breakfast plate, and the soothing of warm water over my hands. I put some hip action into sweeping and made a little waltz of mopping. When I stepped outdoors on my way to chapel for noontime mass, I smelled the tart desert air, turned 360 degrees, not even embarrassed to be imitating Julie Andrews in *The Sound of Music*, and effused, "God, I love you! What a gorgeous day! Thank you. Thank you. Thank you."

Noonday mass is preceded by the Angelus, which means that between three recitations of the Hail Mary, we recite other words, among them, "And the Word was made flesh and dwelt among us," and Mary's famous "Let it be done unto me according to thy word." This morning, I really hear these words and want so much to mean them, to hear what God tries to tell me.

Bells ring three times between passages and crescendo into a final nine rings. After this we sit in silence for a little while, letting it all sink in. This Friday, as usual, I gazed at Jesus on his cross, thinking about something I'd recently read somewhere: "It's our wounds that heal us," and I think, If we didn't hurt we'd have little incentive to change.

This Friday I didn't remain in a half kneel after mass as I do on other days, because on Fridays after mass, we gather at the kitchen table to map out our week's duties. One of the items on the agenda was a discussion about the Sunday after next, when the monks would renew their vows, which would be followed by a potluck brunch. They discussed how they would make their vows in front of the altar in order of seniority, Suzy first, Connie, then Eric. After the meeting, Eric was going to Cup and Sword to make sure there were enough bottles of the champagne they'd brewed.

As they moved on to other items on the agenda, I looked at my friends jotting their notes, flipping their calendars, volunteering for duties, deciding on invitations, and asked if anyone wanted tea. Connie did. I put the water on, dropped Barry's black tea bags into two mugs, and waiting for the pot to whistle, I thought, I can't imagine a better life; I love it here. I thought how sometimes God talks to us through our feelings and intuition. I sat back down with our tea and asked what they'd think of my making temporary vows.

They thought it was a great thing for me to do. But as happy as they were to invite me in, no one really felt equipped to take on my formation, or education; they are only three people and have almost more than they can handle running a retreat center. But Eric did volunteer to give me a reading list, answer questions, and talk to me whenever I needed.

As a lay novice I would join the monks in daily work as usual, and eventually, when they thought me ready, on Sundays I'd rotate in to give the reflection—which is what the homily, or sermon, is called when delivered by a nonpriest; I will take turns ringing bells during the Angelus and bells to announce mass and prayer; I will prepare the altar, light candles; and at Compline Saturday nights, swing the thurible to incense the host while kneeling before the altar; and sometimes I will serve as the "altar boy"; often I will offer wine during communion with the words, "The blood of Christ."

Today, like some of the Buddhists in the seats, I'm dressed all in white, in the same outfit I'd worn to the party after the rape, like a bride. Obviously, temporary vows of only a year are much easier to make than marriage vows meant to last a lifetime. Still, the monks and I have agreed that for this year, God comes first in devotion, my writing second, followed by the community, which means Nada usurps my family and friends, attaining a prominence in my life I could never truly give to a lover.

I am moved as Connie, Eric, and Suzy each take their turn reading deeply felt, even poetic vows they'd written and now recite on their knees in front of the altar, looking up at Christ.

Somewhere in the chapel is one of my best friends, Renee. Her visit was planned months before I decided to take vows, and although at the moment her presence here has flown out of my mind, I consider the timing pure gift. We'd been housemates for three years in the house she owns in Santa Monica. A house that smelled of jasmine-scented candles and fresh air. We loved to give dinner parties and invite a tableful of friends and people we'd like to befriend. I'd cook while Renee decorated, lit candles, then poured wine and kept the conversation going. Sundays we'd read the *Times* in the back garden by the fountain, sipping strong coffee before walking over to the farmer's market down the road. Many weekends we hosted pajama parties with friends who'd flown in from out of town. Weekdays, Renee would leave for the NPR bureau, and I'd leave to write in an office that Jim Brooks, the producer of *Riding*, had given me on the Sony Pictures lot.

I was already in love with Mary then and went to daily mass in Culver City and Sunday mass in Santa Monica. Renee never went to church with me, but she believes in a higher power and allowed me to hang a dozen of my Mary paintings in our shared TV room with the trundle bed. I had big dreams when I lived with Renee. *Riding in Cars with Boys* would be a smash hit; the whole country would know my name; opportunities would tumble over themselves; people who'd thought they were my betters would fill with envy; I would never be shy again because with my newly acquired respect, fear of others would evaporate like a puddle in the sun. Naturally I'd have more money than I could ever spend and one day would probably write and direct a movie of my own.

It's not as though I wasn't ambitious before I moved to LA, but LA is where the ambitions seemed achievable—even imminent. A Mustang convertible had awaited me at the airport the first time I set foot on Hollywood ground. My agent drove me around Beverly Hills in his Mercedes, telling me I'd live in one of these mansions one day. "I know talent and I know people, so believe me when I say, You could own this town." I didn't believe him and I did; it seemed the perfect happy ending to my life story, which had begun with a little girl in public housing dreaming up her own stardom since she was old enough to snap her fingers to a Pat Boone song.

Riding had been in development for eleven years, and by the end of my three and a half years in LA, it had finally been greenlighted for production. I was deep into writing *Looking for Mary* and would leave my work to sit on Penny Marshall's bed, eating white peaches and chocolates, watching the audition tapes of a dozen famous actresses. Drew Barrymore was hired to play me, and Penny began fishing for what I really felt about the script, which I had not written. She was curious to hear my ideas and intimated that she might involve me in rewrites. To be so involved would pull me away from my book, which I thought of as my real work—and as a responsibility given to me by Mary. I was afraid such involvement would tempt me away from God, and from my *new* dream, of a spiritual life. So I bolted. I moved to Mexico, where the Virgin of Guadalupe is as real to people as their mothers.

Part of me wondered if I was too afraid of answered prayers, of realizing my dreams, and so had run away. This may have been part of it. But a bigger part was how much the love of Mary had filled me up, how much happier I was, how hopeful.

It was the right move. It's possible to have success at one's vocation, which for me is writing, and still live a spiritual life. But I wasn't practiced enough. I was barely practiced enough to hang on to God for long in Mexico.

In any case, I needn't have worried. My celebrity never arrived. The movie wasn't a smash hit, and although someone's probably getting rich on the hundreds of times it plays on cable, I'm not.

And now, here I am, a victim of rape in a white dress, waiting to take vows as a lay religious in the Nada chapel.

It's my turn, and I kneel in front of Christ, feeling like I just got a whiff of the first real day of spring, my heart spinning thank-yous, choking on tears. I look up at Jesus, my companion, my friend, my heart welling like it's spring-fed, and I can't stop the tears. My vows blur; the paper is shaking. My whole body is shaking; I can't get out a word.

On John the Baptist's day, the day I was raped, they say in Mexico that the rains come, greening the world back to new life.

I'm in your hands, I say to Jesus. Help me get calm. Help all my tears green me to new life. I breathe deep. I breathe deep again, and I begin in a shaking voice that eventually grows strong, reading vows that differ little from the first vows I wrote more than a year and a half ago:

Thank you, my beloved, for bringing me here to Nada.

I promise to love and work, play and pray, holding you, my God, as the focus of my every day.

I will help to create and maintain this place of retreat, so others can pray in beauty and silence and peace.

I promise to be chaste in body and mind, fasting as much as I possibly can from criticisms, judgments, fears, and worry so that I may love you and every person, animal, and deed that crosses my path more fully.

I promise to be obedient to the Holy Spirit, to listen to the promptings of your will, and to do it.

I promise to live in simplicity, grateful for all you've given me, abstaining from possessing more than I need.

I serve as "altar boy" at this mass, and afterward I stand to the side and offer wine to the line of people waiting to drink. Before each sip, I say, "The blood of Christ," then after a sip is taken, I wipe the chalice with a linen cloth. One time when I look up, Renee is standing in front of me with tears in her eyes, and mine fill again. Without uttering a word, Renee is saying, "This is so right, Bev. I'm happy for you."

Human

If you take little account of yourself,
You will have peace wherever you live.

Abba Poeman

Connie, Eric, Suzy, and I are seated in the chapel after Vespers. I, who have never been any good at all with intimacy and sustaining a healthy live-in relationship, find myself married to three people. I try not to be critical, to blend in, go with the flow (which is God), and to not feel my customary sense of separation and alienation.

Yet I will be cleaning the kitchen during Saturday chores when a retreatant walks in and asks where the brown rice is. The retreatant, who let's say is a woman, will have been shown where everything is during her orientation. I understand how easily such a thing as the location of brown rice can be to forget, yet I will be annoyed, because the retreatant failed to even look before asking me. Really, I will be annoyed because I was interrupted. Even though I know that God is in the interruptions. Even though I know I'm called to treat every visitor, heck, every person anywhere, as Christ.

If it were Connie, Eric, or Suzy, let's say it's Suzy this time, she would not only tell the retreatant where the rice bin is, she'd pull out the drawer, ask if a container to hold the rice is needed, and then retrieve one. Then when the retreatant, finding Suzy so friendly, strikes up a conversation, asks a question, perhaps mentions what she's planning on cooking, no matter what Suzy had been in the middle of doing before the interruption, she will be absolutely present and interested. All the monks would be.

I might try to act as though I were, but my act wouldn't convince anyone. And besides, I'm trying to be genuine and not wear a false face. So usually I show them where the rice or whatever is and go right back to what I was doing.

I'd hoped when I made a commitment to a life of prayer that the act of making such a commitment would short-circuit my transformation into a loving and patient, kind, compassionate, selflessly generous woman; I'd become a clear wire through which God's current can flow. I want to be Paul on the road to Damascus, struck blind, utterly transformed. Ha! I'm more like the crippled man who crawls to the healing pool for years and years. Christ does finally show up and cure the man, though. And I hold out hope every day, all the time. Meanwhile, transformation is work. Transformation is a minute-by-minute choice, and I forget to make the right choice from minute to minute. If transformation were a job, I'd be fired.

I am so self-involved, I embarrass myself.

It helps when I remember to pray, again and then again, "Please, help me to bear serenely the trial of being displeasing to myself." Now, Vespers is over and instead of standing and bowing and then leaving in silence, as usual, we all just sit there. Eric, who has been staring, I think, adoringly at the huge crucifix, says, "That chest has always bothered me. It's out of proportion."

"I can't stand his thighs," says Suzy.

"I've always hated the color of the carpet," says Connie.

"And those stained-glass windows," I say, inexpressibly relieved to finally vent. "Who designed them? They're hideous."

"They're seventies," says Suzy.

"It was Tessa," Connie says. Tessa, the cofounder of the community, was abbess for many years and is Connie's older sister.

"I love the crucifix," I say. "The expression on Christ's face. It's so—I don't know."

"Yes," they all agree.

I spot a cobweb between Christ's hair and his hand and plan to climb up and sweep it away with a broom. "I love this chapel," I say.

"Me, too," they all say.

Now that the gates have been thrown open for criticizing: It has always bothered me that there's no Mary in our chapel; well, according to me there's no Mary in our chapel. According to Suzy there's plenty of Mary in our chapel. We are seated in the kitchen at our weekly Friday meeting following mass. We've all made ourselves something to eat and have our calendars and notebooks in front of us. I have brought up the lack of Mary's presence, because it has been troubling me for a while and I've finally found the courage to say something. Suzy points out that there's a Guadalupe. She's two feet tall, standing on half a globe, all clay, and hollow, so a lighted candle inside can shine through little cutouts. You may have seen one just like it. They're all over the southwest. The clay Guadalupe is low on the floor in front of a wooden column of the same color and can be seen only when you enter the chapel—if you even notice her. I argue that Carmelites are devoted to the Virgin, aren't they? Shouldn't Mary not only have a presence but be a focus in our chapel? Suzy counters with "She's in the stained-glass window."

This makes me go apoplectic. The two stained-glass windows are so ugly that in one the Sangre de Cristo mountains are depicted as blood red, and in the other a woman in jeans sits on a rock with a dog that looks suspiciously just like her, while on her other side, her crying two-year-old is trying to climb onto her knee.

"Every woman's the Virgin Mary? You're the Virgin Mary, I'm the Virgin Mary?"

Suzy does not react except to remain calm and continue to look at me.

I understand the impulse to depict Mary as everywoman. She was a poor village girl who delivered the Magnificat, a cry for equality, for lifting up the lowly and sending the rich away empty. She delivered her baby in a manger.

But my impulse is to show her as Queen of Heaven, an everywoman transformed into God. Or as God who became an everywoman. I do understand that calling Mary God is a heresy. But that's how I think of her, so disembowel me. Obviously, God cannot be known and so can't be truly pictured, but if you must, and many must—because as Jung said, "Images hold the power to transform much more than knowledge does"—then depict her as awesomely lovely, on a cloud, wearing a fabulous queenly gown with a train held by angels. Or depict her as she looked back when she walked the earth as an everywoman, in the costume of her day.

Eric, the peacemaker, suggests that we might get a statue for the courtyard.

"That's the *courtyard*," I respond. "It's *outside*. We need Mary front and center. I want to look at her when I'm in the chapel."

"But where?" Connie, the practical one, asks.

She's got a point. There isn't exactly any space.

Our talk takes place during my second fall. Near my second Christmas, Rita, the woman hired to clean out and restock the hermitages after retreatants leave, shows us a painting she did of a young Virgin Mary.

Because it's Christmas, the anniversary of Christ's birth, but also of the Divine Mother's giving birth, Suzy arranges to borrow the painting. In front of the lectern, she and Connie have set it on a music stand, which they've draped with a lovely scarf that flows to the floor. The painting depicts Mary from the waist up; Mary's hands are clasped in prayer, her head bowed. Bits of glued-on paper make a pattern on her robe. It's a beautiful painting. Mary is deeply serene in it, and when I look at her, I become serene.

Many people remark on how much they love the painting, how nice it is to have Mary in the chapel.

Bernadette, a friend of the community for decades, buys the painting and donates it to the chapel. Suzy is not happy, but when Connie and Eric, who like the painting, too, agree to hang it on the wall beside the lectern, Suzy says, "I'm not the only one who lives here. I'll adjust." Underneath the painting is a wooden ledge. Rom Loti, the leader of the local Hindu ashram, donates a lovely turquoise scarf to drape over it. I donate a ceramic candleholder, a strip that holds five votive candles. But the candles drip onto the scarf, so Suzy, who can hardly bear their existence because they are so tacky, bows to necessity and buys electric votive candles anyway.

When a friend presents the monks with a gift of two hundred dollars to "go and have some fun," they instead buy a sculpture by a local artist to adorn our Mary altar. At first the sculpture is not to my liking on the altar. It's abstract and shaped almost like a squashed paper bag that's open at the top.

Then, eventually, even though the sculpture is blue and white, it seems to me like a heart, dented and creased, sat on and crunched, but unable to ever close.

Cold World

It's the Sabbath, a day of rest, a gorgeous, sunny winter Sunday. The roads are clear and free of ice, and I plan to go for a walk, looking, as Gerard Manley Hopkins put it so beautifully, for "the deep down of things." But back in my hermitage after mass and a heavy brunch, the easy chair beckons. I doze off and am startled awake by a thump and a squeal. I see through the side window a little bunny charging up the hill in a flurry of sand, tufts of fur floating. As my heart buzzes with adrenaline, I've an eerie feeling there's more to see, and it's the reason I'm here and not hiking.

My legs feel stuck in cement as I drag myself to the window. Up the hill beside the hermitage about ten feet away stands a giant hawk, its wings spread along the ground as wide as a car fender, its head tilting and rotating, its hawk eyes scanning. Suddenly it jumps, or is it a stomp? It does it again then pulls a large dead rabbit dangling by its shoulders into the sky.

I slam my palms to my eyes, "No no no no no no no," I yell, stomping back and forth, trying to be an eraser.

But I talk myself down: I tell myself, God wants you to see this. I open my eyes.

The hawk has lowered the rabbit onto a patch of snow on a north-facing hill thirty yards away. It's standing next to the carcass, lifting one leg thick with white feathers and shaking it as though something's stuck to its claw, then lifting the other and doing the same. Next it shrugs its shoulders and tilts its head from side to side. It repeats the sequence maybe a half dozen times before hopping on the rabbit and tearing off hunks of fur then flesh.

This is what I say to God: *Are you kidding me?* I was awakened from sleep by a rapist, remember? Did I really have to be awakened today by a murderous raptor? Are you trying to traumatize me into facing the ways of the world you made, where every living creature is a victim of, eaten by, other living creatures—except for people. We kill one another for the fun of it. You said the meek shall inherit the earth. What I want to know is, When?

A few days later, it snows during the night, and at dawn I see a baby bunny, which must be the one that escaped in the flurry of sand. Now it occurs to me that the dead rabbit was its mother. The little bunny's at the edge of the wooden platform outside my window, facing me, its ears pinned to its head, its eyes half closed. It's numbingly cold out, and the bunny sits there in the snow all day without moving—not even to twitch its nose. When it still hasn't moved by the next morning, I conclude it, too, is suffering from PTSD, mourning its mother, near comatose from a broken heart, mortally depressed, too sad to live.

The next morning it finally opens its eyes, perks up its ears, and turns them like antennae. I follow their direction and see, on the top of a pinyon tree, the hawk! I grab my hair and stomp back and forth again. All this little bunny wants is to eat and hop and shit and pee and one day have sex. I've never seen it even close its eyes, because if it relaxes for one second it could be mauled to death. It probably never even sleeps. I look at the bunny, its eyes big; I look at the hawk, its beady eyes scanning.

I think, I'm witnessing the law of the world, the law of nature. The hawk has to eat. It can't help being a carnivore. I should not intervene. But then I think, I don't care. I'm part of nature, too. I charge out the door, the screen bangs against the house, I run into the snow in my slippers toward the tree, flailing my arms, hissing, and the hawk flies away.

Even though I'm a part of nature, too, I do not leave food out for the bunny, because I've been instructed not to feed wild animals because they will then become dependent on you, and no longer be wild.

The bunny perks up. It hops around and nibbles plants. When it snows, the bunny makes a little burrow in it; when there's no snow, it makes a burrow in the same spot in the sand. I look for the bunny as soon as I wake up; I look for the bunny when I return from prayer, or chores, a hike, or anywhere. From its tracks in the snow and the sand, I see that it wanders off in every direction and sometimes shelters under the platform.

The bunny and I never interact, yet the little rabbit is my treasured companion all winter. Until one sumptuous May twilight. The winds have died down, the air is rosy from the sunset, and the bunny stands five feet away, facing me, which it has never done before. I'm at the window with the light on, wondering if the bunny sees me. Whether it's been aware all along that I've been its friend. Because, I could swear, it's looking at me.

It stands on its hind legs, stretches its ears as tall as they'll go, and then elongates its face as though it's printed on silly putty. The bunny stays like that for what feels like a full minute, then charges to the right; stops on a dime; charges to the left; charges back to center, jumps high in the air, and stands on its hind legs facing me again, stretching its ears and face. It remains that way perfectly still for a half minute. Then it zigzags first this way then that, and repeats the whole sequence all over again: a rite of spring, a mating dance, a dance of pure jubilation, freedom, adventure, joy? And then it runs into the prairie.

I never see it again.

Here's the thing: It's easy to see God in a bunny.

Here's the other thing: It's just as easy to see God in a hawk.

Family Crisis

If we look at each moment
As a point at which we meet God
And make it always a moment of love
and surrender to his will,
then each moment of our lives
can and should become one
in which we seek and find God.

Cardinal Basil Hume

Like the little bunny, my mother had a mother who died when she was young. All my life, if I asked my mother something like "Are you going to so-and-so's baby shower?" she'd answer, "If the good Lord doesn't take me first" or "If I live that long." To my reaction, she will respond, "You never know."

My mother's in her mid-eighties now and only in this past decade has death taken a seat for real. My mother's had emphysema for almost fifteen years, has been on oxygen for the past eight, and for the last few, she can barely walk to the bathroom without getting winded. I've told her I love her; I've told her I'm sorry I've been so critical, sorry that I never told her enough how grateful I am for all her help and love and support, all my life; I've asked if she has any regrets; to tell me her most cherished memories; who among those who've died she misses the most, and why; I've asked her to watch over me once she passes; and I've asked if she's afraid to die. "Yes," she said. "Of the unknown."

I consider myself prepared for my mother's passing.

Still, when my new cell phone rings before sunrise and I see my sister Janet's phone number, I'm stung with dread. My mother has had a massive heart attack, was shocked twice, and is on a respirator in the intensive care unit of Yale New Haven Hospital. She's been given a 30 percent chance of making it, and the next forty-eight hours are crucial. The nurse my sister spoke to recommended that the family gather.

I'll be heartbroken if I don't get to say goodbye. I call my father and cry, "I just want to see her one last time," and he says, "We all want that, Bev. We all want that."

Connie drives me to Alamosa, promising prayers, and by 1:00, I'm on a flight to Denver. After making a connection, and many pleas to God to fill me with love enough to give to whoever needs it, I arrive at LaGuardia late at night and take a cab to Brooklyn Heights, where my son and Jessica are waiting. Jason has baked a bag full of chocolate chip cookies for us to take along and serves me a plate of warmed-up baked ziti he made for dinner. Jessica will stay in Brooklyn with the kids; I now have two grandchildren. Three-month-old Audrey was born this summer. I'd babysat three-year-old Zachary while his parents went to the birthing room at the hospital, and then I accompanied him the next day to meet his baby sister. I'd had the collapsed stroller, gifts, Zachary's hand to hold as we entered the hospital lobby, and I spilled a bag of nuts and dried fruit all over the floor. Zach said, "It's okay, Nana. Accidents happen." And I knew his parents were doing an excellent job.

It's hard to be so near Zach and Audrey yet so distant. I peek in on them as they sleep, bend to smell their scents as I kiss their cheeks, then Jase and I walk to the garage, retrieve his car, and leave. It's well after midnight, and I-91 is deserted and as dark as driving through a tunnel. My son goes eighty and ninety, and I'm glad for the speed. It's 2008, early fall of the general presidential election. Jase tunes into right-wing radio to hear what the other side's saying, then gets incensed. I suggest music.

The intensive care unit is so bright it could be noon on the equator. We're directed to a room to the left midway down the hall. The door is open, and I see my sister Janet alone sitting at the side of my mother's bed. My mother's so bloated from the fluids being pumped into her, she looks like a beached sea lion. Monitors blink and beep, tubes and wires run into her arms and groin; a respirator tube is down her throat, and a large clear oxygen mask is strapped to her face. Jan stands as we enter, and my mother's eyes grow large as those of a three-year-old who's about to be handed a begged-for popsicle. She mouths our names around the tube in her mouth and lifts her arms in a gesture of "Come close." Which we do, to kiss her.

She is deathly pale and more animated than I've seen her in years.

There are bruises on her swollen arms and legs.

Jason looks like he might cry.

Which makes me act as though everything's fine. My mother just had a massive heart attack; she may die and she may live; all shall be well all shall be well all shall be well.

Janet, Jase, and I are the only family members at the hospital. My brother and father had followed the ambulance, then, because it was too much for my eighty-five-year-old father, they'd gone home.

That first night, Jan and Jase leave, and I pull up a chair and hold my mother's cold hand, which seems strange. My family is not physically affectionate, yet my mother and I must have held hands all the time when I was little. I am so grateful to hold her hand, and to have it feel natural again, that tears fill my eyes.

Nurses walk in and out all night, checking monitors, prodding my mother. The fluorescent light glares like aluminum. My mother dozes in short snatches then snaps awake, fists clenched, a look of terror in her eyes. I tell her she was a good mother. "I never for one second doubted you loved me, Mom. I know that couldn't have been easy. Sometimes I was hard to love."

She makes a face like she just bit into a lemon and shakes her head.

I tell her I love her, and she mouths that she loves me, too. I kiss her cheek, I stroke her hair. I try to distract her with chat about my grandkids, how good Zach is at hitting a baseball, how big he and Audrey looked when I saw them sleeping, how Zach loves preschool, and how when one of the ten students in his class is absent, the others send the absent child a kiss from their hearts. I've brought rosary beads and ask if she'd like to pray a rosary with me. She says she would, and I finger the beads, praying the words aloud. My mother closes her eyes, and soon she's dozing. I complete the rosary then stand over her, close my eyes, and pass my hands a few inches above her body, imagining golden light from God flowing into the top of my head, then down through my hands and into my mother.

St. Paul spoke about the gifts of the spirit, how each is given a special gift, for the common good: the utterance of wisdom, the utterance of knowledge, faith, healing, miracles, prophecy, the discernment of spirits, speaking in tongues, the interpretation of tongues. He goes on to say that just as our body cannot only be eyes, so as a group, as the body of Christ—or you could say, as humanity—we need all the different members, with all their different gifts. I would love to have the gift of miracles but will be grateful, indeed thrilled, with the utterance of wisdom through my writing. And at four o'clock in the morning at Yale New Haven Hospital, confronted with my mother's failing body, just for a little while, I'd like to be given the gift to heal.

I imagine the gold light as God's peace, warmth, love. I'm picturing the golden light embracing, surrounding, penetrating my mother's hurting heart when I feel a tap on my arm.

"Stop," my mother mouths. "You're scaring me."

"Sorry." I pull away my hands.

This was not the first time my presence at the side of my sick mother scared her. Seven years ago I got word that my mother had stopped eating and came home to find her trembling on the sofa. She'd lost so much weight her bones showed through her clothing.

"She don't do nothing," my father said. "She won't move."

"I don't want to," she said, not defiantly, not stubbornly, simply stating a fact, which is not something she'd normally risk in front of my father if it meant opposing his wishes and chancing a flare of temper.

"Why are you shaking?" I asked.

"I don't know. I'm nervous."

"About what?"

"Everything. You."

"Me?"

"Your visit. I don't know, I don't know, I'm confused. The doctor changed my blood pressure medication; maybe that's it."

I called her doctor. I called an internist friend. I called a psychiatrist friend. The consensus was that depression masks as many things, and that my mother, who has a history of it, is likely massively depressed. My psychiatrist friend recommended she see his mentor, at Yale New Haven Hospital.

When I suggested him to my mother, she said, "I'm not going. I'm not making your father drive me that far."

I dropped the subject. Each time she stood up to go to the bathroom, she groaned. When my father brought laundry in to her so she could fold it as she sat on the sofa, she tsk tsked her tongue and shook her head as though having a silent complaint fest with socks. This behavior was not that unusual. What was unusual was how I was in the room and she wasn't complaining out loud. I made pasta, and she didn't join us at the dinner table. Or eat on the sofa. She was dying. I had no doubt.

In desperation I looked in the Yellow Pages under "Geriatric" and to my surprise found a geriatric psychiatric clinic in the next town. I called and spoke to a therapist named Mrs. Marino. I described my mother's condition and read to her all the medications my mother was taking. I told her it was possible that the cocktail of medications might be responsible for her current collapse, but that I believed she was severely depressed.

Mrs. Marino suggested we make an appointment for the day after tomorrow. When my mother arrived she would first speak to Mrs. Marino and then be evaluated by a psychiatrist. If my mother were accepted into the program, and it sounded like she most likely would be, a commitment would be required. My mother would be enrolled in their outpatient program, for which she would be picked up in a van four mornings a week. Treatment would be from 9:00 a.m. till 1:00 in the afternoon. Lunch would be served.

"How much does it cost?"

"Is she on Medicaid?"

"Yes."

"Then it's free."

I had no idea such services existed in the United States. (Due to lack of funding, the clinic closed a few years later.)

There was still one problem. I'd been trying to get my mother to go to the senior citizens' center for ten years, and it had been like trying to get a cat into a carrying case. "She'll never do it."

Mrs. Marino replied, "It's my job to convince her. You just get her in here and leave the rest up to me."

I sat next to my mother on the sofa. "Mom," I said, "I found a clinic at Memorial Hospital." I told her that she had an appointment the day after tomorrow to talk to a social worker and a psychiatrist, who would review her medications and maybe prescribe something to help her feel less depressed. "It's for older people," I said. "That's who they treat."

My mother blinked and said, "Okay."

On the appointed day, we walked slowly to the car, my mother taking baby steps, and found that the passenger window had been left open during that night's rain. Because the seat was soaked, my mother sat in the back. Driving along, it felt like my mother were my child in her car seat, sitting quietly, looking out the window. It was May, and fruit trees and azaleas were in bloom. "Look, Mom," I said, "how pretty."

"Mmmmm. I hope my allergies don't act up."

"Sometimes it helps to decide that you're going to notice the beautiful things, you know, Mom? I think we get into a habit of looking for trouble, concentrating on things to worry about. We forget to be grateful."

I shouldn't have lectured, especially to a person in the middle of a deep depression, who'd spent a lifetime, nearly every waking moment worrying about money, her children, what would happen or not happen tomorrow, the weather. Still, most of the time, I believe in change, in transformation; I couldn't call Christ my teacher if I didn't.

I looked at her in the rearview mirror. My mother looked frightened.

At the hospital, I accompanied her into the social worker's office. Luckily the social worker was chubby, smelled like bath powder, laughed like someone was tickling her, and wore a lovely pink-and-violet, Laura Ashleyish flowered-print dress. I could tell my mother felt more comfortable than she could have imagined, because Mrs. Marino was one of us, meaning Italian, plus, she was a Mrs., and she was fat. When I was a kid, my mother, a first-generation Italian American, used to deliver her own version of St. Paul's gifts-of-the-spirit talk. She'd tell me, her most avid audience: "It takes all kinds," and enumerate the different characteristics of people of different nationalities—which one could call prejudice—but lots of what she said was true. Here's what she said about fat people: They have big hearts, good senses of humor, and when they dance, they're light on their feet.

After a few factual questions, Mrs. Marino asked my mother if she'd be comfortable speaking to her alone. And my mother agreed.

As I sat in the waiting room, everybody who passed by smiled big and said hello. Before I could complete a rosary begging Mary to mother my mother, Mrs. Marino called me back in. My mother, Mrs. Marino said, had joined the program—the whole package, four days a week, four hours a day, lunch included. Then Mrs. Marino led us into the office of Dr. Rossi, who unfortunately—because he was another Italian and therefore likely a shoo-in—was out of town at the moment. Dr. Fields, a woman, was filling in.

As we sat down I asked my mother if she'd rather be alone, and she shook her head, no.

Dr. Fields took out a yellow legal pad and asked how my mother was feeling. "Lousy," my mother said, then meekly covered all the bases: no appetite, tired all the time, flushing—from a medication, she thought.

"And how is your life? Are you happy? Are you content?"

"Not really."

"Has anything happened lately to upset you or make you unhappy."

"Not that I can think of. I'm bored. You know. There's nothing to do but watch television."

"And your childhood? What was that like?"

She shrugged and looked vacant as though she couldn't think of a thing worth saying. "Fine."

"Mom," I blurted. "Your mother died when you were twelve, you and your brothers and sisters were put in an institution. You lost your whole family. Your baby brother, Anthony, died. (Of TB, like their mother. The last time my mother saw him, he'd stood in his crib in the hospital, begging, 'Please, Don't go!') You had a horrible childhood." I'd been crying about her childhood ever since my mother cried to me about it, beginning when I was three, and probably before, but I was too young to remember. I can still cry about it.

But when I brought it up now, my mother looked as though I'd just tried to explain a trigonometry equation. "It wasn't that bad," she said.

I begged to differ—until I realized I'd just awakened from a thirty-year sleep in which I'd never noticed that my mother had stopped mentioning her childhood. Now, it seemed, she'd forgotten it.

Dr. Fields looked at me as though she were not the least surprised, like she'd witnessed such selective amnesia before and had empathy for my shock. "Do you have anyone to talk to about your feelings?" she asked my mother.

"Not really. I can't talk to my youngest. She's too emotional, she'd get too upset. And I never could talk to Patty. I could talk to Beverly, but she lives in Mexico."

"But she's here now and she brought you in for help."
"Yes. She did."

The next day she was dressed and waiting when the van arrived to pick her up. That afternoon when my mother returned, we made tea and sat at the kitchen table as she filled me in. There was a whole group. But first she met with Mrs. Marino alone, who asked if she believed in God and if she asked for help.

"What did you answer?"
"Sure."

Then there was group therapy, which included a black woman named Bertie. "Full of hell," my mother said. "Bertie said, 'I'm spirited. I talk a lot and I appreciate it if you all would tell me to my face if I'm getting on your nerves and don't go talking behind my back. Anything you got to say, I can take it.'"

"I love that," I said.
"Me, too."

Suddenly, my mother had a social life.

Back home in Mexico, I called my mother to ask how she was. "Your father looks at me funny," she said. "But I don't care. I believe in psychiatry."

Then she told me about the recovering alcoholic. "Such a mess. Cries all the time. I feel bad for him, poor man. He said he used to be a professor at Yale. He says his kids come home to visit and tell him he hit them when they were little. But he doesn't remember doing it. Do you think he did?"

"Probably," I said. "People tend to want to forget pain. Because it hurts."

Years before her breakdown, at the urging of my therapist, on a visit home, I'd told my mother that she'd hit me as a child. "I never laid a hand on you kids," she said.

"You hit us with the wooden spoon. You pulled hair, you pinched, you slapped across the face."

"Oh, Bev." She shook her head. "I don't remember. But if I did that, I'm sorry."

I regretted having said anything.

And was comforted now because I'd a feeling that not only had she forgotten hitting us, she'd forgotten my accusation.

But then, I'm not so sure I should be comforted; I'm not sure at all that forgetting is good for the soul.

I understand how the forgetting can begin when we're still children, to survive abuse, to endure crippling fear, to relieve our own perceived guilt. I suspect that blocking painful events makes us prime candidates for dementia in later years. Not blocking them out might be what Christians call carrying one's cross.

Therapists have told me from interpreting my dreams and observing certain behaviors that I was abused when I was young, and possibly still in diapers. This is not something I want to believe. But not long ago, I was given the gift of a massage for my birthday. The masseur was a man, and as I lay on my stomach with my palms facing upward at my sides, he leaned his genitalia into my cupped palm and I had no idea what to do. I didn't know if this was okay or not. I did know I felt uncomfortable, but I didn't know if it was okay to feel discomfort, or if my discomfort was a good enough reason to move my hand away—or to demand of him an explanation of what the hell he thought he was doing.

I am told that this kind of confused passivity is common among women who have been sexually abused at an age when they couldn't tell what was okay and what was not, when adults were assumed to always do the right thing.

I wonder if I was raped to help bring the earlier rape or rapes into consciousness. I wonder if the earlier rape or rapes have risen up to bite me.

But right now, at Yale New Haven hospital what I and my mother may have repressed is the least of my worries. My mother, I am told, has blood in her urine. Not uncommon, but not good, either.

The next morning when Jan arrives, she's brought my father, who last saw my mother as she was being lifted into the ambulance at their house. "Buddy!" my mother mouths, as excited as a kid.

"Lou," he murmurs, leaning over her, rubbing her belly in a circle.

My sister and I leave the room to give them privacy.

My siblings and I work well together. My sister and I hold vigil. Janet stays through the days and I through the nights until I become too emotional from lack of sleep and we switch. My mother is never alone. Pat and Ed and their spouses visit daily, often twice in a day. My father visits daily, too. The parking garage is a hike so we ferry him to the door, and we make sure that at least one of us eats dinner with him every night. We meet with the hospital staff, ask that a pulmonologist be called in. We take notes, ask questions, do research, and make demands. We are shocked to find that the doctor in charge of my mother's case is an intern, doing the cardiac section of his training, and thinking he'll probably end up a pediatrician. My sister Jan and I are convinced our mother would not be alive without our advocating for her. If Janet had once been too emotional, she isn't anymore. My eyes are the size of golf balls from crying while my sister is clear and calm and admirably rational.

I am more intimate with my mother's body than I've been

since I was a baby. The hairs in her nose, her toenails that need trimming, the bruises on her limbs, her breasts when she's given an electrocardiogram. I swab her false teeth with water when she needs moisture. I feed her ice cubes, hold her hand, pat her leg, walk in right after she's shit her diaper. I kiss her cheek. My mother's helpless as an infant, and as with an infant I can touch and caress her. And she likes it.

She has a wristband: "Louise Donofrio 6/14/23." My mom, born on flag day all those years ago, a child of the Depression, an orphan, one of the last of a generation that soon will be gone from the earth.

Loving hurts, and loving can increase your openness to pain and suffering. Loving God has been good practice, as has gazing at Christ on his cross almost every day for a few years. One of the messages of the cross has to be the transformative power of pain. Pain precedes death and new life. Is there ever *not* pain before change, before recovery? Can there ever be gain without loss?

I consider it a gift that a week before I got the call, as though to prepare me, I'd been on a silent eight-day retreat to our cabin St. John of the Cross, a thousand feet up the mountain, with no electricity or running water except for the nearby mountain stream.

As I left for retreat, Eric had said, "Let yourself be loved."

And I had, from the hummingbird mistaking me for a flower to the sparrow on a difficult hike to an alpine lake above tree line. I had gotten lost finding the trail, was tired and aching and thought I could not go on. Until a sparrow feeding in the branches of a tree separated from its flock, hopped to the edge of a limb a foot away, and studied me as I studied it, for three minutes. Exactly the reminder I needed, that I am not alone, that I'm as much a part of the mountain and this little bird as my huffing lungs and rapidly beating heart are part of me—and that miracles are everywhere if you slow down long enough to notice. I remembered that the mountain had called and was calling still. How when I'd arrived at the cabin I'd felt that the trees knew I was there as much as I knew the trees were there, that my mere presence affected everything around me, as everything around me affected me. I remembered how Christ said if you have faith the size of a mustard seed you can say to the mountain, "Move," and it will move. My faith was not strong enough to tell any mountain to go jump in the ocean, but it was strong enough to tell myself I could make it to the lake. And I did.

During the week up on the mountain I kept finding big rocks that had moved, the evidence of their footprints right next to them—and no footprints of bears that might have turned them. A reminder of mystery, of the depth in darkness, the profundity in not knowing.

At my mother's side, every day I pray that my mother not suffer or be afraid, and that God let her go peacefully. I hold her hand and tell my mother that when she goes Mary will be waiting for her, arms wide open. I tell her that her own mother, whom she hadn't seen in seventy-two years, whom she'd still missed so keenly when I was a child, will be waiting for her, too. All her dead friends: Franny Vanski; Rose Stupski; Cleone Plunsky; her favorite sister, Antoinette; her baby brother, Anthony. "You'll see them all again."

I don't know if dead people are somewhere waiting for us. And I don't know for certain that Mary will be waiting, either. But I do have faith Mary will be there, and that Mary is mother and friend enough.

I don't pray for this, but I wish God would let my mother die. She has asked, "Why doesn't the good Lord take me? Why is he keeping me alive?" She has lamented, "This is no life." And I agree. Twelve hours on a couch watching television every day, laboring for each breath, would make me jump out a window. Death is inevitable, why prolong the wait? But my mother lives.

She stays in the ICU for ten days, then is moved to a hospital room where she remains until she's strong enough to enter a rehab facility at a nursing home in our hometown. Jan returns to New Jersey to tend to her family, and I make arrangements to stay a few more weeks, wanting to see my mother safely settled into the nursing home, and to be able to cheer her on in rehab at least for a few days before I return to Nada. Pat and Ed live in the same town as my parents, so I will not be leaving them alone.

> Clearly, great pursuers of the spiritual life
> Know that the secret of the spiritual life
> Is to live it until it becomes real.
>
> Joan Chittister

My father and I have been housemates, politely dancing around each other for weeks. My father is a hero. He not only has stepped up to the plate, he's excelled at being the househusband and the nurse. Still, we've been antagonists over the years, a cop and a rebellious daughter, whose animosities have been relieved by many respites. And during this respite, we are profoundly getting on each other's nerves. His hovering when I cook is driving me mad. I'd thought that my life of prayer, my life lived in silence, all the love I receive and am trying to give, the extraordinary peace I've experienced for two years have made me a more calm, and if not an enlightened person, at least a person in control of her temper. I have not, however, become less emotional. I have cried during this election, hearing on the radio in my hermitage the raw hate at Tea Party gatherings. I cried when witnessing John McCain being so snarky in debates, pandering to people's fears. Calmer the morning after, I realized the man reminded me of my father, specifically of the time I confronted him at the urging of the same therapist who'd counseled me to confront my mother. I'd said, "I feel like you don't respect me."

"I respect you, what are you talking about?" he said in a disrespectful tone.

"You were mean to me, never trusted me, always thought the worst. You hit me—"

"You deserved it."

That stopped me short, both because of his sparring schoolyard tone and because I probably did deserve it.

But later when I recounted this conversation to my mother, she said, "You were just being a teenager."

And I caught myself: I'd readily adopted my father's wrong judgment of me, which, because he was a cop—and society's enforcer—I'd interpreted as society's judgment of me. And then I used that same judgment to judge myself—wrongly. I was so angry at my father we didn't speak for a time.

My sister Jan called near Christmas that year and said, "Dad lost sight in one eye for a day. How are you going to feel if he dies and you're not speaking? What are you going to do at Christmas, not come? Not see everybody?" She didn't accuse me of elder abuse, but she could have.

I called my father. "Dad," I said. "I want to—"

"Let it go, Bev. Please," he pleaded. "Let it go."

And so I had.

Now, when my father, a lifelong Democrat I know to be a racist, refuses to tell me who he will vote for, I'm certain he's about to turn coat and vote Republican.

I insist on asking him every day. And he insists on not telling.

Then one evening, as I'm clearing the table to do the dishes, he takes an apple from the refrigerator, turns toward the living room, sing-songing as he leaves the kitchen, imitating and making fun of Obama, " 'Change, change, change.' Nothing ever changes."

I blow up. "Oh. But *you* change, don't you? A lifelong Democrat, and now you're going to vote Republican before you die, and disappoint me." Then I just had to stop and listen to myself. *Disappoint me?* Was that what my judgment about him had always been about? He didn't measure up to *my* expectations? *I didn't respect him?* The apple had not fallen far from the tree. Christ was clear on the subject:

> Do not judge,
> so that you may not be judged.
> For with the judgment you make,
> you will be judged.
>
> Matthew 7:1–4

I think it was Father Richard Rohr who said, "God's greatest ally is what is." Not what should or could or will be. Not what was. But what is.

I follow my father into the living room, determined to love him, and to begin the practice of What Is. "Hmmm," I say to myself. "My father won't tell me who he's voting for." I sit with this for a minute, then ask, "Feel like some tea?"

I wait until my mother is in rehab in a nursing home close to her house before I depart. The morning I leave, tears fill my mother's eyes. "Thank you, Bev," she says. "I don't know what

I would have done without you. I never knew you'd help me like this."

Neither did I. Whether it was from love or blood or both, something primal was activated. The same thing happened when Zach was born. Far from being duty, helping was pleasure.

Change

Who Says an Ant Can't?

> And deliver us from evil, Amen.
>
> The Lord's Prayer

My first retreat to our little mountain cabin, St. John of the Cross, happened in the fall, before my mother's heart attack. That first time, in late September, the weather was glorious, wildflowers nodded their heads, crickets jumped everywhere, leaves fluttered on trees musical with birds. This time, it's mid-March, cold and gray, the flowers and crickets long dead, and the only birds I ever see are a pair of tuxedoed magpies screaming as they streak by.

The community agreed to abandon our hermitages to make room for a group of Sufis who come every spring, and I am not thrilled. Contributing to my sinking mood is a book I've brought with me for the seven-day retreat—a treatise on meat-and-potatoes Catholic theology—as dense as its print is small, much of its content impossible for me to believe. Eric suggested I read the book because I'd begun rotating in on Sundays to give reflections and had recently made a faux pas—otherwise known as a heresy. "Christ is a man, I mean God," I'd said, when dogma clearly states that Christ is "all man *and* all God." I knew this, I just said it wrong.

Still, I need to be clear on the church's teaching if I'm to continue giving reflections. So, up in the cabin in the clouds I read this book, which claims that God condemned all of mankind for Adam's sin. That Satan was an angel who wanted to be as God and so he fell from grace straight into hell and took a bunch of other angels with him. When Adam, who had free will, committed the first sin of disobedience and ate from the Tree of Knowledge because he also wanted to be like God, God bolted shut the gates of heaven and condemned all mankind to suffering. Which makes the God described in this book the same God I fled from with fear and loathing in my heart as soon as I was old enough to think for myself.

This God, who never changes, is all perfection and knows everything that's going to happen. This God already knew when Adam sinned that God would give mankind a second chance by sending his son, Jesus, to suffer and die for our sins—to make reparation, pay the price of his life, and redeem us into salvation. Just as one man, Adam, had condemned mankind; one man, Jesus, would rescue it, the gates of heaven would be thrown open, and we'd have eternal life.

I knew this doctrine and could bear it only by refusing to think about it. I never thought I was required to actually believe it.

I'd been eager to read this book because I hoped it would enlighten me about evil. According to the book, it's we people who created evil, which I've heard before, and the explanation still doesn't satisfy.

The simple truth is that I am not all that clear about what I believe. If you ask me, I'll say, "God is love." If you ask me what

I believe about Christ, I'll say, he walked the earth and was God come to live among us in the flesh. He came to teach us how to be, by example. Through the Cross he showed us how to transform pain. I might say that God sent Christ to show us that we are loved. I will also say that we all have Christ in us, and with God's help, we too can become a Christ. I might also say, I believe there have been on this earth people who have achieved this, and for all I know there are a few of them kicking around right now.

Mostly, I avoid such discussions. I am no intellectual, and arguing about God does not increase my faith; in fact, it has the opposite effect. The last thing I want to do is debate about something that is illogical, ineffable, and for me, mostly experiential.

I've an atheist friend who for a while insisted on debating me, in a monologue. She says that separating the dark from the light, splitting off the dark by insisting that God is all light creates most of the problems in the world. All things are light and dark. Once you say one person or nation or belief system is right and good and another is wrong and bad, you've created opposition and division. And a justification for punishment and war.

I couldn't agree more. I'd shrug in answer. "But God is love."

I know this because I *feel* God's love. Now, thinking more deeply because the theological book has demanded it of me, I have to say, God is love but maybe God isn't all good, the way we, who were supposedly cast in God's image, are not all good. Dark has to exist for light to exist, evil has to exist for good to exist—and vice versa. And this is the only simple thing about it: Faith is not logical and God cannot be explained.

I have brought along no other book to read on my retreat, and the weather is too miserable to escape the cabin for more than an hour or two at a stretch. Only a quarter mile up from here, the snow's so deep, I sank to my thigh when I tried walking on it. In the cabin are one Bible, a book of St. John of the Cross's collected writings, and a field guide for birds. Tucked between the latter's pages is a list of twenty-two birds I spotted on my last stay here. I try to reason with myself that my sinking mood is more about the weather than what I am being asked to believe.

When a sunny day finally arrives, I'm out the door the second the sun hits the cabin windows. It's gloriously sunny and clear, almost 40 degrees with no breeze. On the northern slopes, snow glitters like tinsel. But the southern slopes are dry, and as I weave my own tracks through their yellow grasses, I run my fingers along the tips of pine needles, branches tap my shoulder, and the deep piney fragrance enters my pores. I step over a big pile of some large animal's crap and, when I see no seeds in it, wonder if the animal is a carnivore. I sit on fallen trees and notice how their roots, boulders and rocks tangled in them, leave abscesses in the earth where they'd so recently reached and grabbed and hung on.

In a field I encounter a magnificent ponderosa that died many seasons ago, collapsed into a heap of branches and sticks dry as bone. It had started as a tiny seed, and soon it will be dirt, soon it will be part of the earth it had grown from. Clouds mingle and pull apart, a stream rushes over rocks shattering sunlight into winking crystals, and I feel such love for this mysterious, hurting, glorious world God made, I weep. I sit on a rock in the sun and eat nuts and dried fruit, drink the water I've purified from the stream. I am so grateful my heart is tender and huge.

Then heading up a hill so steep I sometimes have to grab the tall grasses to gain purchase, I almost touch the leg of a deer or an elk, red with the hoof still attached, recently killed. It's a shock that feels a betrayal to the beauty of the day, a blow to my heart, which deflates like a punctured balloon as a sob shakes every inch of me. A picture of the mother rabbit dangling from the hawk's claws comes uninvited. So does this thought: When the baby bunny ran off that last time, it never came back because it was eaten. Beauty and ugliness coexist around me, everywhere I turn.

I trip on rocks on my way to the cabin. I use up all my tissues and wipe snot with my sleeve. I blow my nose onto the hem of my sweatshirt. "How could you?" I rail at God. "Why?"

To the book on meat-and-potatoes Catholic theology that says people created evil, I say: We may be cruel and torture one another, but who invented illness? Who *created* suffering? We may have invented weapons of mass destruction, but who invented hurricanes, earthquakes, tsunamis, tornadoes, floods? And I'm supposed to love a god who did this out of a need to punish?

God either loves but cannot protect us; is all-forgiving and exacts penalties, yet loves; or is indifferent, paring his nails as children die in wars they didn't create and are raped and tortured to death. None of these Gods appeal to me, yet I love God and I feel loved by a God I do not and can't possibly know.

Back at the cabin the sun has dipped below the horizon, and it's dinnertime but I'm not hungry. Last time I was here on retreat, I left the blinds open at night so I could be dazzled by the starry sky. I did this even though from the deck I saw people every day hiking up the trail. This time, when the chances of someone's sneaking up to peek in the windows are as great as a bear's knocking at the door, I've closed the blinds every night, blocking out the enormous shivering sky. And I close the blinds again tonight. Then, feeling claustrophobic as usual, but now also angry, I defy my own fear and open the blinds. I turn on a gas lamp, sit down, and decide I'm not going to finish the book on Catholic theology; I'll leave Nada if I'm required to believe what's in it.

Then I spy an ant hauling a dead fly up the glass. Sometimes the ant pushes the fly's body; sometimes the ant turns around and pulls it. Halfway to the top, the ant and its dead fly fall all the way down to the windowsill, and then the ant begins the climb all over again.

The ant reminds me of something Penny Marshall said. We were at a dinner hosted by the movie's producer, Jim Brooks, who stood to make a toast, which went something like, "To Beverly, our favorite slut; without her we wouldn't have a movie to make." Penny leaned across the table and asked, "How does that make you feel, being called a slut?"

"Fine." I shrugged. It was a joke. There was a time when the term applied.

"See?" Penny said, turning to the screenwriter, coaching him on another rewrite, "She's like Sisyphus pushing that rock, pushing that rock. Knock her down and she gets right back up."

She was right, I think now. That's me. Since the rape I've been pushing that rock, pushing that rock—toward God, toward healing—hoping against hope, hoping contrary to experience that God isn't going to push me back down so hard again.

Back at that dinner, I'd formed a picture of a Joe Palooka punching doll—hit it and it bounces back—which seemed a perfect image for life. Unless you give up, or decide to lie down and die, you get smacked, and then you come back for more.

The ant never gives up and finally, I guess, learns a lesson. It changes strategy and decides to drag the fly laterally across the three windows. Eventually, it makes it to the rough-hewn wooden wall, where it can climb more easily. It lugs the fly to the crack where the wall meets the ceiling and disappears.

This thought comforts a little: If you're willing to try a different way, sometimes your climb gets easier.

I wonder if I might have to find my own way, if I can be a Catholic who must range further to go deeper. For the first time I wonder if I will not again renew my commitment to Nada.

The next morning, a day shy of when I'd planned to leave, it's snowing, which presents the very real danger of my being trapped up here for days. I'm relieved for the excuse to leave early, clean up the cabin in record time, pack everything up, and head down.

Back at Nada, the Sufis have left early, too, to make it over the passes. Eric is alone in the kitchen sorting through their food leavings, dumping small jars of salsa into one jumbo jar, doing laundry. I join in the work, happy to be busy. After a while, I make us some coffee, pour two cups at the table, and sit with Eric, who asks, "How was your retreat?"

"I can't believe everything in that book," I blurt. "I can't be a Catholic. I may have to leave. I used to believe God is all love, but I can't think that anymore. That book says God's all 'perfection.'

"But if there's evil in the world, which there is, then God had to create it. Whatever's in the world has to be in God. There's evil in me, there's evil in you, and there's evil in God. There has to be."

Eric looks at me kindly. "I should have never sent you up there with that book. It can get intense on that mountain. I didn't mean you had to believe every word. I don't believe every word. Every theologian has a different theory, and you're entitled to yours."

"That's a relief." I giggle, breathe, and then burst into tears. "How do *you* explain evil? How do *you* think of it?"

Eric told me that he believes God created creatures who can create. And we created evil.

This is not so different from what the book on Catholic the-ology said. But while I'd felt like burning the book, I don't feel like slugging Eric. In fact, I wish I could believe what he believes. And I do believe what follows: Eric says that God loves us always, and Eric believes that God's will changes to take into consideration our choices. Eric could not offer an explanation for the suffering we people do not inflict on one another—such as the calamitous violence of nature or illness—but he does believe, as I have always wanted to, that one day the lion will lie down with the lamb. And it will be our doing.

I think of a cat I know that never hunted in his whole life, or killed another creature. I believe he was evolved and that there are other cats like him.

I've read of rats being trained to ring a bell to be fed, and how the rats' descendants, as well as rats with the same genetic makeup in other parts of the world, learn to ring the bell in fewer and fewer tries with each succeeding generation.

I've heard of an experiment done in Washington, D.C. A group of people prayed for six weeks straight, and the crime rate decreased by 23 percent.

I need to believe that we're all evolving, that every living thing can and does change, including God, and if we don't destroy the planet first, we may one day live in peace.

"Do you ever doubt God's existence?" I ask Eric. "That we just make God up because we want to believe there's some meaning in all the suffering and pain?"

"Oh, I have faith." Eric leans back in his chair. "I believe in God. I think of it this way: Would we have hunger if there wasn't food?"

This may be as good an argument for God's existence as I've heard.

I receive Eric's faith that day like honey from the rock.

But I'm not done with contemplating evil—and apparently it's not done with me.

Messengers

The monks have gone to Denver for a few days and left me alone at Nada, which is a first. Two people arrive, one on Friday, the other on Saturday, needing to talk to someone—about evil. It seems no coincidence I'm the only person on the premises.

The first, whom we'll call Rebecca, is a retreatant, who looks absolutely pleasantly normal. Her face is open and clear; she's wearing a hunter green, crewneck sweater, jeans, sturdy leather hiking shoes. Her chestnut hair is long and thick and shiny; her green eyes brighten when she tells me she's a warrior, "High, high up in God's army," and has been sent by God to the San Luis Valley on a mission. A decisive battle between good and evil is gearing up for the not-too-distant future, and right now, the San Luis Valley is a battleground. She also says she just returned from a mission in China, has three thousand nuns praying for her in India, and doesn't yet know what God wants her to do here. And even though she's terrified— "There's a lot of evil around, can you feel it?"—she's surrendered her whole self long ago and has no more will of her own, only God's. "I'm His instrument. All I do is listen. Pray and listen. Then do what He tells me. God is Everything," she says. "EVERYTHING. So powerful. Bev! You've no idea."

I'd taken her through the customary orientation, showing her where everything is; we'd returned to Agape from the chapel and are seated on one of the benches along the vestibule wall. She asks whose pictures are hung here, and I point: "St. Teresa of Avila, St. John of the Cross, St. Thérèse of Lisieux."

"Holy, so holy," she says. "Can you feel it?" She's been talking for two hours and now announces, "You're not a nun," even though I don't remember having mentioned this. "What are you doing here, Bev?" I tell her shortly about the rape and the monastery tour, and my decision to make vows as a lay member nearly a year ago. She tells me that she's been raped, too, a few times and received excellent therapy at a center in Arizona dedicated to healing victims of rape.

Her conversation is disjointed. She lets drop that she went to law school, has a masters in theology, has been institutionalized seven times, was a Baptist minister in the South for two years, and her wealthy Connecticut family won't allow her to step foot in their house anymore. "I gave it all to God, man. There's no more me, just His will."

I am aware that she may be crazy or at least in the middle of a manic episode. Her energy is magnetic, and I find it hard to end the conversation. When we finally do part, she asks me to pray for her. "There's so much evil in my cabin, I hardly slept last night. The bed's in the corner. Demons love corners. There were too many. I couldn't get rid of them all. I had to sleep in the chapel."

The next day, Rebecca calls from the road to tell me that she'd left shortly after our talk. This means she'd truncated her retreat by a few days. She was calling me from a motel in Alamosa. She's on the road, she said, doing detective work around the valley, and will return to Crestone, but she's not sure when.

That afternoon, not an hour after I hung up with Rebecca, I'm leaving Agape when a man we'll call Jared speeds up in a white truck, hops out, and asks if there's a priest he can talk to.

"Sorry, no. He's away."

"A nun?"

"Sorry, it's just me."

"Do you live here? Do you pray every day? Are you Catholic?"

"Yes."

"Can I talk to you, please?"

We take seats in the housemaster's office downstairs, and he opens with, "Are you familiar with satanic possession?"

"I've seen *The Exorcist*," I say as my heart begins to vibrate like tracks under an approaching train. Jared is startlingly good-looking, a Marlboro man, with a long ponytail, polished cowboy boots, and turquoise eyes.

"I thought, Who can I talk to? The Catholics. You're the only ones who'll deal with evil. I called the bishop in Pueblo, but I'd have to wait till next week to see him, so I drove over here."

There's a satanic circle in town disguised as a shamanic circle, he says. He knows someone who is involved. "She thinks she's a white witch. She thinks what she's doing is white magic. But the leader is satanic, passing herself off as a shaman. And my friend can't see it. I doubt any of them do. She's getting pulled right in."

"But your friend's probably only trying to do good for people. We pray for people all the time, ask things for them, right?"

"All you can do is pray for God's will."

He's right. How can we ever know for certain what's "good" for anyone, including ourselves—or "bad," for that matter? The Buddhist parable "Good Luck, Bad Luck, Who Knows?" doesn't come to mind at the moment, but it could have. It's a well-known story, and if you've heard it before, feel free to skip to the next paragraph. A farmer is given a horse, and his neighbors say, "Such good luck." The farmer replies, "Good luck, bad luck, who knows?" His son falls off the horse and breaks a leg, the neighbors say, "Such bad luck." The farmer replies, "Good luck, bad luck, who knows?" The army comes around conscripting soldiers for war, and the farmer's son is exempted because he has a broken leg. Good luck, bad luck, who knows?

"Evil always comes disguised as light, pretending to do good. That's how they can do the most damage, you see. They know I know them. I can spot 'em a mile away. And they can tell. Look at these eyes." They look wild and icy cold. "You know they've seen things." And then he makes his eyes go back to normal again.

"Why can you spot evil, do you think?"

"It's my penance."

I want to ask him "for what?" but restrain myself and ask him how he's going to fight evil.

"You can't fight evil, you can only throw love at it"—a response that makes me think he might not be crazy or paranoid. And then, as though he's read my mind, he says, "Of course, I could be crazy. Do you think I'm crazy?"

"Could be."

He laughs. "You're all right."

I walk him back to his truck, where he thanks me and tells me I have a good heart. Then he hugs me hard and says, "I love you," which scares me as much as anything else he said.

I'm eager for the monks to come back, which they are expected to do that evening for Compline—not a moment too soon. We maintain silence after Compline, so my news has to wait until after brunch the next day. After we've cleaned up after brunch and the retreatants have dispersed, I tell Connie and Eric and Suzy about the visitors.

Connie says, "We've seen our share over the years."

"Two in two days?"

"Well, no."

"Don't you think it's a little bit strange that they came to talk about evil when I was the only one here?"

They seem to agree. Or at least they didn't disagree.

Eric says that the man probably really needed someone to talk to and did feel love for me because I listened. Nobody had anything to say about Rebecca, besides to shake their heads, which I resent. I don't want to believe Rebecca is crazy. I would love God to send warriors around the world to battle evil. Besides, in their own times, weren't most of the prophets considered out of their minds?

A few days later, I'm lying in *savasana*, corpse pose—a deep rest at the end of a yoga practice, which is supposed to mimic sleep without your falling asleep. I hear a noise, open my eyes, and a man is pressed against the floor-to-ceiling windows, looking in.

I sit up and he runs off.

This is as close as it can get to a man's invading my house and waking me from a deep sleep. My heart hammers so hard it propels my body to the door. I step outside and see three men by the barbed-wire fence that borders the Nada property. "Excuse me," I call.

"Sorry," one of them says. "I thought it was empty."

I remember that one of the monks had mentioned a while back that workers from Fish and Wildlife would be replacing the fence one of these weeks, and I assumed the week had arrived.

The monks don't lock their doors, and neither did I after the first time I stayed here: I'd locked myself out of Gandhi and had to disturb a lot of people to find out where the extra key was stored. So I never locked a door again, until now. Now I lock my door every night, terrified the man will return.

I'm not sure exactly when, but within the next few days, I arrive at the chapel to pray the rosary with a small group of women and see Rebecca sitting cross-legged on the floor with her eyes closed. She doesn't join in. Then when the women leave, Rebecca and I step outside and sit on a bench to talk. She tells me she's been all around the valley investigating, and that the Native Americans and Mexicans—"You know, the ones who were here first"—won't touch Crestone with a ten-foot pole. According to Rebecca, native peoples believe Crestone is a portal, where spirits pass back and forth between this dimension and another. (A few years later, I'll read an article in the local paper about lineage holders in Tibetan Buddhism visiting Crestone, who say that evil energy gathers in the saddle between the peaks of Kit Carson and Challenger.)

Rebecca says she saw an enormous flying saucer with blindingly bright lights two nights in a row, hovering. Then she repeats a story I'd heard before, that charred animal bodies are sometimes found in circles in the prairie, where there are no tracks of either people or the animals.

Rebecca pats my arm. "Thanks for listening, Bev. Not many people will, you know."

I tell her about Jared and the Fish and Wildlife intruder. "Shit, they're trying to mooch your light. Come on." She stands up. "You need protection. We're going to secure your house."

I'm not sure what the monkles would think about this, but I don't care. I bring Rebecca to my hermitage, and she speaks in tongues. She splashes holy water in every corner, on every window, and sprinkles it on my bed; she tells me I'm exposed to the whole valley because of my wide-open view. "Do you even know what kind of danger you're in?" She splashes holy water around the outside perimeter of the cabin then sprinkles salt. She tells me that demons can come in through electrical outlets and telephone lines. She says that every night before sleep I must sprinkle holy water on my bed and pray for protection. She informs me of my three guardian angels. When I'm in danger, or frightened, I should call on them by saying, "Holy, holy, holy."

I'm terrified.

She tells me that God has spoken to her about me and told her I'm a mystic and an intercessor. "Do you even know what intercessor means?"

"That I pray for people?"

"God's gathering his people. And you're one of them." But aren't we all?

She instructs me to pray on the beads of a rosary, " 'I humbly and sincerely accept you, God, as my father,' and then on the next bead, 'I humbly and sincerely accept you, Jesus, as my husband.' Really pause and feel every word, even if it takes you hours. This is *your* prayer. You have to accept them. You have to let them love you. Believe it, feel it, they love you so much."

I try this a few times, but my associations with "father" and "husband" are too negative, so I give it up.

I don't know where Rebecca stays in Crestone; I suspect her car. She tells me that from midnight till four in the morning, she goes off to specific locations, where God has directed her. I don't know what else she does, where exactly she goes, when and how she eats. But I do know she prays in the chapel, where we seem to run into each other every day. Then one morning, after a week or so, she claims to have succeeded in her mission. She says the two gigantic flying saucers with blinding lights returned, and were landing. "I didn't do it. God did. All I did was listen. But somehow, because I was there, they didn't land and then took off. Bev, I cracked the case: There are people in Crestone claiming God's glory for themselves. People never learn." Rebecca shakes her head.

Hardly news. The surprise would be if there were no glory-grabbing spiritual leaders in a town that's home to twenty spiritual centers. "The brighter the light, the darker the shadow," as Kay said about Nada's founder on my first visit.

I bid Rebecca goodbye in the driveway. We hug, then she types her number into my cell phone as she reminds me again to always keep holy water in my hermitage.

When the dust of her bumping-away CRV has long settled, after I've locked the door and slept with the light on for two weeks straight, this is what I think: Rebecca is touched by God, perhaps; she is mad, perhaps; or she was both. But this is the one thing Rebecca is for certain: afraid.

"Do not be afraid" is the most repeated phrase in the Bible.

The nighttime terror, my fear of the dark, of intruders, my dread of my nightmares and of the bogeyman that lingers in the room after them—in other words, the fear I've experienced since I was raped—is not different from the terror I experienced as a kid when I'd flip the light switch by the door and quickly make a fly-ing leap into my bed. Because I was afraid a man, the bogeyman, hid under my bed, ready to reach out and grab my ankle.

There was nothing rational about it.

And there is nothing rational about the terror I've experi-enced since the rape, either.

The warped unconscious logic of my terror:

I was raped once, which proved I *can be* raped—which means it's entirely possible to be raped again.

But it was always possible to be raped.

Truth:

As my mother is fond of saying, "You never know. Anything can happen."

Anything can happen at any time. That's life. Good luck, bad luck, who knows?

Living in fear because anything can happen at any time, liv-ing in fear of life—of suffering—is crippling.

At any birth there is pain.

This is what makes us grow: great love and great pain.

Don't run from the pain: Doesn't Christ on the Cross tell us this?

+ + +

Here's what I've been thinking, here's a plan of sorts:

When the real-life bogeyman, the rapist, came to my bed, I was terrified with good reason but kept my head. To try to get rid of the rapist, to work on his sympathy, I said, "I'm going to be sick," which was a lie. But then I actually did feel sick. Next I made myself tremble for dramatic effect. And then the trembling became real, too.

That night with the rapist, nauseated and trembling, on the verge of losing control, I stopped myself. I got a grip, because my instincts told me it was the smart move.

Perhaps it's not even desirable to give up fear entirely, but it's certainly desirable to give up my fear of the dark and of evil, and maybe of suffering. It may not be possible, but I plan to begin trying.

One more thing:

I have been afraid that the figure in my nightmares was not merely a representation of evil, but an actual evil entity.

Now, when I go to sleep at night, I ask God to help me with this, to give me some illumination.

And I have a dream. I'm on the outside of my house, looking in at a large shadowy figure. I do not know how to get back into the house, and I'm frightened. I don't know who this figure is, how it got in, how I can possibly get it out, or if I can even get inside myself now. In any case, I'm too afraid to even try.

I have a spiritual-direction session on the phone with Estrella to discuss this dream. She is silent and asks if she can relate the dream to her spiritual director, Father Paul. I give her permission, and we speak again a day later. In the course of our talk, I come to this conclusion: "I think the dream's trying to tell me: If I keep thinking about, focusing on evil, it'll take up house, and be impossible to get rid of."

"I'm so relieved," Estrella says. "I didn't know how I was going to get you to this realization, but you got there. You got there. Yes. Yes. Can you see how this is true?"

I can.

St. Antony, the first Desert Father, lived alone in a cave and was attacked every night by demons, beaten bloody, black, and blue. This was not his imagination; people witnessed his wounds. He lived in fear of the demons until the day he realized that the only power the demons possessed came from his own fear. Now, when the demons came, he laughed at them, and they slinked away.

Redux

It happened in 2006, on June 22, John the Baptist's day. I'd just been surfing the Web, looking for a place where I could renounce the world, topple my ego, and grow my true self from the seed of God inside me.

I already loved and worshiped Mary, and wanted to love her son, too—to understand what Jesus' life and death meant. I was headed for a monastery.

It seemed a cruel joke; after I'd bookmarked a monastery to bring me closer to God, the town's demon slips into my bed. I said, "Now, God, now?" I said, "Why, God, why?"

Almost three years later, I ask, "Why the rape, what am I to learn?" I ask this every night before sleep.

Near dawn the answer comes in the same words with which my father taunted me about Obama. Change, Change, Change erupts in the sky, booming like fireworks, flashing like light-ning.

I was afraid the rape would change me forever and I'd never again be the same person. Was I nuts? I was so great? Why the hell wouldn't I *want* to be changed by a powerful experience?

God might have more to tell me, so I keep asking, "Why the rape? What am I to learn?"

I have another dream. The phone rings, I pick it up and hear, "RUN!" But there's no time to run before an explosion rips through the house, whirls me off my feet, whips me through the air. Blinded by dust and debris, not knowing if I'll live or die, I say, *"I love you God I love you God I love you God I love you so much,"* choosing to trust, having no choice, my heart growing calmer.

After the rape it was just like this dream.

I believe God gave me this dream to show me a life, my life, lived in faith.

I realize that I now know what I didn't know before the rape: My faith is unshakable.

Now the three-year anniversary of the rape is only a week away, and I'm leaving to visit in Brooklyn and then to teach. The night before I leave Nada, I call Zach, who's almost four. "I'll be there tomorrow. I'm so excited!"

"Me, too!"

"It'll be really late when I get there; you'll be sleeping and won't be able to see me. But in the morning, will you come in and jump on me? Give me a great big kiss and hug to wake me up?"

"Okay. I will. Here . . ." He hands the phone back to his fa-ther. As far as phone conversations go, this was a long one.

I have a key and let myself in after midnight. By the time I've unpacked and eaten something, it's two in the morning, and I'm so tired I have to force myself to change into pajamas.

Then in the morning, although it doesn't feel it at the time, I am given a blessing, an antidote to the big bang that three years ago launched me into this new life, a nudge to remind me that all is well, even better than well, beautiful.

I'm sleeping so deeply at dawn I've no idea where I am when Zach bounces his body onto mine, and I scream so loud I scare myself even more than I already am. In his pajamas printed with cars from the movie *Cars*, his hair tousled, his legs so much longer than the last time I saw him, five months ago, Zach is straddling me, sitting on my belly, a smile still there but fading, wondering if I'm serious.

And I am serious, seriously going to get over being frightened and rescue this longed-for moment, enjoy every second of this boy's presence. I give him a bear hug and rock him from side to side, crooning, *"Mi nineto*, my darling, my sweet, I love you, I love you, I love you so much. It's *so good to see you.*"

"I love you, too," Zach says, facing me, expectant.

"Want some breakfast?"

Normally he resists all meals, but this first day he'll do anything for me, and I for him. "Okay," he says. "I think we have some Monster Munch."

We hold hands walking to the kitchen. I fix his cereal then place the bowl on the dining room table and sit across from him, intent on his every mouthful. I hear Audrey, who will soon be one. She's talking baby talk and is being carried up the stairs by her father, my son.

I turn to smile at them and hold out my arms.

Poco a Poco

When I return to Nada it's nearing Our Lady of Mount Carmel's feast day, July 16, time to renew our vows for another year. I'd forgotten all about the plan to renew them at a mass, followed by a celebratory potluck, and now, on the ride home from the bus station, I object to it. Why, I ask Eric, who'd picked me up, did I have to profess my promises in public, when they were between God and me? Eric, the de facto leader, although he resists the role (which helps me to trust him), explains that we profess them to the larger community because our vow-taking is a gift to the community, that anyone who professes a Christian life, which at its essence means loving your neighbor, is a gift to their neighbors.

I argue that I'm still not very good at loving my neighbors and I pretty much failed to keep the promises I'd made in public the year before. Making these promises feels like a New Year's resolution announced to the world. Eric replies that promises are aspirations and the best we can do is try. Then, because he's a reasonable and nice guy, he promises that next year we can revisit the subject.

As before, during a crowded mass, after the Gospel, one by one we kneel in front of the altar. Being the baby of the community, I go last. As soon as I look at Christ's face, I fight tears of gratefulness again. When I'm finally calm enough and before I read my vows, I say what I hadn't thought of till now: "My Love, my vows haven't changed from last year, and last year I pretty much failed to keep them. I know you understand how weak I am, and how much I need your help."

Afterward at the potluck, a half dozen people thank me for my commitment. Some tell me I made them cry when I said that I'd failed. "Because we all do."

Maybe forty have come to the potluck, but the crowd feels huge, probably because small talk is required, and small talk to me feels like giving blood. This time, I'm pleasantly surprised by actually enjoying most of the conversations.

Still, I'm thrilled to see that, except for a few people, the crowd has left by noon. But then the three people stay on. And on. The monks and the three people and I sit at the kitchen table. I am not interested in the conversation, not in the mood; I am talked out. As I watch the stove clock digits change, I start to turn mean, picking apart what people are saying, their expressions, their clothes. So I escape to the library before it gets worse and lie on the sofa, plotting how I can most expediently leave. It's Sunday. I want to hike, maybe do some weeding in the garden, there's that book on Nureyev I'm dying to get back to. Last year, in the same situation, I might have accomplished the escape, but this year, it's impossible. It wouldn't be fair to Connie, Suzy, and Eric, who could be as tired of talk as I am but would never, ever show it and certainly never leave until all our guests had.

Feeling a headache threatening between my brows, I return to the kitchen and sit down. Then—I may have only imagined this, but I swear—a breeze quickens through the window, and I remember to pray.

"Hey," I say silently, "Jesus, I need some help here." And the Jesus prayer springs to mind, so that while I listen to the chatter, part of me prays, "Lord Jesus Christ, son of God, have mercy on me, a sinner."

I may be imagining this, too: The room grows brighter by twenty watts.

Although I still would rather have been off enjoying my day, I hardly mind the conversation now; perhaps it's improved because I ceased to be a scowling presence at the table. I smile and respond, and the smile isn't an act in the thespian sense of the word.

Later that night, Connie, Suzy, Eric, and I gather to celebrate our vows with leftovers and a glass of wine. They discuss a man who'd had a few nervous breakdowns, how he'd looked a little crazed at the potluck and could not hold a coherent conversation. But the man had rarely stood alone, because our community is so kind and so many people had made a point of talking to him.

I hadn't even noticed the man.

I have made a birdbath out of a terra-cotta platter. Whole flocks of mountain blue birds come to bathe and drink from it. A dozen birds will be on its rim with forty more on the ground waiting a turn. All at once, for no apparent reason, the whole flock will suddenly lift up en masse and jet to a nearby tree. There will be one bird left on the ground, looking at them, befuddled.

I think, if I were a bird, that would be me.

"You guys are so kind," I say. "I wish I were." And then I tell them how hard it had been for me to sit at the table for that extra hour. "You'd never even have considered plotting to leave like I did, would you?"

"It's a spiritual practice," Connie says. "We've been at it a long time. It gets easier."

"And, hey," says Suzy. "You didn't leave, either."

"I wanted to."

"But you didn't."

That night I fall right to sleep. Sometime in the night, a hot flash wakes me up just as outside my window a flash of heat lightning lights up the pinyons, and grasses, the sunflowers and hill that seem to say, "Hey."

Trophy

Does sunset sometimes look like sunrise?

Rumi

It's time to puzzle together a book and make meaning from these past few years of my life. The monks make allowances for me. I no longer serve as housemaster; I do continue to cook brunches, shop in Alamosa, pick up and drop off retreatants, but less often. I go to prayer most days, although my presence is not required. This book will not only take concentrated time, it will take strength and wisdom I don't yet possess. Physically, it will require the use of every cell still functioning in my brain, which will require eating and sleeping properly. I drink green smoothies every day; I take to standing on my head.

Intent on the writing, my year flies by, and again in June, I visit family and prepare to teach.

This time, I bring Zachary, who is almost five, to see my folks. The first time I brought him with me, he was one year old and my father had held Zach's hands, bent his old knees, and danced with him to a jingle on the radio, "Bababa, bababarino, Babarino Pontiac." Now Zach is kind enough to give his great-grandparents a kiss and a hug apiece, but he's eager to play, and before I go out back to pitch him a ball, he agrees to help carry our things upstairs to the room where we'll spend the night. For the first time, Zach notices the gaudy gold crucifix on the wall. "Look, a trophy!" he says.

I haven't taken Zach to church since he was two and ran amok, pulling out bulletins from the backs of pews and throwing them in the air. For some time I said grace before meals but felt like people were indulging me and worrying their food was getting cold. So I stopped.

I did keep praising and thanking God, and was now wishing I'd conducted some sort of dialogue with Zachary. I try not to laugh at his mistake and say, "That's not a trophy, that's Jesus on his cross. It's called a crucifix. Some people believe Jesus is the son of God."

"My parents don't believe in God," he says.

"I know. But I do."

"I don't."

I want to present him with a question that will get him thinking, something that will open up the possibility. But I don't have much time, and all I can come up with is the first thing the nuns taught me: "Well, who do you think created everything?"

"The future."

"The future made you?"

He nods, and I wonder if this has something to do with predestination or if he's intuited some law of quantum physics that's beyond me. When Zach was three he could do a hundred-piece puzzle he'd never seen before in five minutes. He adds and subtracts four-digit numbers, and by the time he's six he'll be figuring out square roots.

I don't pursue the future angle and try to get closer to the point: "I like believing in God because knowing that God loves me makes me feel loved. And I like to thank God for things, too, like dinosaurs. And you can ask for help. God loves to help you."

"Everything just is," he says impatiently. "It just is."

He's right, but how to explain the mystery in "just is"?

How to "explain" anything? God just is, life just is. As St. John of the Cross said, "Of God himself nothing could be said that would be like him."

Lately, I get pleasure out of not knowing. Lately, God, who is an "it" to me, seems pure abundance; a beneficent energy, whirling, penetrating, moving everything everywhere; a wind chiming through the trees, All is well, all is well, all is well. Even when it doesn't seem so God is lavishing us with love that's up to us to allow.

Part of the experience of loving life and loving God is accepting that evil and good, beauty and ugliness co-exist.

Of all the lessons to be learned from Christ's suffering on the cross, this from Richard Rohr resonates right now: "We must transform our pain or we will transmit it." Christ took the evil that was done to him, and that's all he did, he took it. And then he forgave, which is what he asks us to do: Forgive life, forgive God, forgive ourselves, forgive the pain. One day, not yet, I begin to send the rapist white light, every day. For him, for myself, and for the world.

As Estrella says, "Terrible things happen that make us shake a fist at God. But God has asked us to help grow the Kingdom of God. We can grow bad things—fear, envy, cruelty, hate. But God still runs the universe, and God is bigger than bad and is dissolving bad poco a poco, to whatever extent our consciousness will allow. That's what God sent Christ for, to ask us to do greater things: With every good thought and feeling, we're helping God grow good things."

I look at the universe: Our sun, one of billions in our galaxy; our galaxy, one of billions in the universe.

I think of seeds buried in the dark.

I think of spring.

+ + +

At Wilkes, on a panel I hear myself telling students that I write memoir because I'm drawn to the truth, that truth is illuminative. "It gives light to the world. And it heals." As I say this, I know I must read the scene of the rape, a scene I've been writing and rewriting and am finally satisfied with. The evening of the reading, as I wait my turn, one of my colleagues mentions that yesterday was the beginning of spring, and I realize that today is June 22, St. John the Baptist's day, and the fourth anniversary of the rape—the first anniversary I have not remembered.

After Words

Father Richard Rohr says: "Jesus was not sent to solve a problem but to reveal the heart of God."

I would say the same about the suffering the rape caused me: It revealed the heart of God—so how could I not be grateful for it? And becoming grateful for experiencing the thing I feared as much as death has made me try to be grateful for every hurt and sorrow, disruption, disappointment, injustice in my life. I try to see how they have made me grow, what I have learned from them.

> When I am weak
> I am strong.
>
> St. Paul

I've a friend whose parents went to great lengths to shield her from pain and disappointment. This is my favorite anecdote about her: As a kid she'd had her heart set on a pony being raffled at the local five-and-dime. When she didn't win it, her father hunted down the winner and bought the pony for her. I always thought my friend the lucky one. When we were in graduate school she had a car, a house in the country, and a room at the Chelsea Hotel, while it was a hardship for me to come up with five dollars to chip in for gas.

She was the friend I called, hysterical, when in graduate school a famous author flunked my thesis—an early draft of *Riding*. I called this friend crying on a pay phone when I was fired from my job as a copy editor on a hot new magazine. Those days, more often than not, it was hard to get out of bed.

Recently, my friend has experienced some terrible blows, open-heart surgery and the suicide of a loved one. My friend is having a hard time getting through her days. Recently she said to me, "I used to feel so bad for you. You were always crying, you couldn't write, had no money; you'd gotten pregnant so young, had to struggle to go to college, you had Jason to care for. You were scared all the time. But it made you strong. You hardly even worry anymore."

Another friend had a body I would have died for. While most of us have to watch what we eat, do aerobics, play tennis, walk for miles, jog, my friend never exercised for a minute and could eat anything she fancied without gaining an ounce. Now my friend's middle-aged with fifty extra pounds she'd like to lose. But she can't resist sweets, limit portions, or make herself exercise. "I have no willpower," she laments.

She never had to develop it because of what we'd always considered a gift: her effortlessly beautiful, thin body.

If you are silent, you will have peace wherever you live.

Abba Poeman, Desert Father

I feel that way myself; God will be my home wherever I go.

Someone once said the faith walk is like an ellipsis: moments of intensity followed by apparent absence. There is no one conversion experience; it is more a conversion of life. Pearls of wisdom, moments of grace strung together. Just as a new phase of the journey had begun when I retreated to the monasteries, so a new stage has begun with my strengthened faith and my healing. I've decided not to renew my vows for the third year. It will be sad to leave the monks, the wilderness, the life. But I do not plan to leave behind the silence and solitude, my spiritual practices, God. The life I create will be centered on them.

I develop a plan, which I share with the monkles. This year my sixtieth birthday, on September 23, will occur on both the full moon and the equinox, one of two days in the year when light and darkness are equal. I want to be at Nada on retreat at St. John of the Cross for that. A month or so later I'll leave to spruce up my house in Mexico and put it on the market. I acknowledge something I've resisted admitting till now: I will never again live in the house I'd built and loved in Mexico. Why would I? I was raped in it.

The money I make from selling the house will set me up in my new life. I'll buy a car and place a down payment on a house somewhere closer—meaning absolutely no farther than a day's drive—to my parents, my son, his wife, and my grandchildren. I will lock my doors at night; maybe I'll plant vegetables, fruit trees, flowers; my grandchildren will stay over for weekends or weeks at a time; we'll bake goodies and make popcorn, watch movies, play hide-and-seek. Friends will visit; I'll visit friends, and I'll go on adventures. I'll make retreats at Nada. I'll learn to line-dance, buy a pair of cowboy boots. Maybe I'll take up hula-hooping. I'll pray, do yoga, and pranayama, and meditate every day. With my gray hair and wearing my new green tights, I'll be silent for stretches, I'll listen, watch my thoughts, talk to God, and beg for help. I will finish this book. And mostly, I will try to embrace whatever ruins these perfectly laid plans.

They go out, they go out, full of tears,
Carrying seed for the sowing;
They come back, they come back, full of song,
Carrying their sheaves.

Psalm 126

Acknowledgments

From the bottom of my heart I want to thank: my angel agent, Gail Hochman, who once said to me, matter-of-factly, "I never pass up an opportunity to do a good deed"—for all these many years of kindnesses, fierceness, and help. Everyone at Viking/ Penguin, especially Carolyn Carlson for responding so enthusiastically to the beginnings of *Astonished*; it was her encouragement that made writing it less daunting and sometimes enjoyable; and to Beena Kamlani, whose brilliance I would like always to shine on my work. My old friend Georgian Lussier and my newer friend Cheryl Waschenko, without whose insights I'd probably still be trying to conceptualize and propose this story. Sara Pritchard, a holy woman in disguise—or perhaps from another planet—for being my best audience, reading everything I write, and convincing me she enjoys it so well that she makes me want to write more, so she can read it. Robin Tewes, my forever friend, for her patience with my impatience, her persistent questioning, her love and help in so many ways, so many times. Caren and Dave Cross, who were there to call in the middle of the night. Bob Mooney, a fellow seeker and God friend whose encouragement lit the way. My fellow writers at Wilkes University whose work has inspired me to reach higher and go deeper. My parents for their steady love and earthy fortitude. My sister Janet, whose tender presence in the world feeds me heart and soul. My son, Jason, for the sweet center of him, his generosity, good taste in choosing a wife, good choice in being the stay-at-home dad, and his open-door policy—to me. Jessica, whose true heart, bright mind, clear energy are everything I could ever want in a daughter-in-law. My grandson, Zachary, who lights the air. My granddaughter, Audrey, who at three already shows what it means to be rock solid. Estrella Morningstar for her wisdom and for modeling a life lived instinctually. Suzy Ryan, Eric Haarer, and Connie Bielecki, for giving me a home where love lives and where I am always invited to the table. To all the people who maintain places of silence and retreat so others may leave the buzz in their lives to be still, listen, and feed their souls. Thanks to the nuns, priests and ministers, the Buddhists and Sufis, the unaffiliated and the regular folk—all of my fellow retreatants—who collectively became my family of seekers. To all the angels and saints, dead relatives, and dead writers, who listened to my downright pleas for help and poetry.

In short: thanks to the grace of God.

Further Reading

This book, heck, my life would not be possible without the books that continue to be the wind at my back, written by mystics, theologians, philosophers, spiritual teachers and pilgrims: *The Sayings of the Desert Fathers*, Various. *Life of St. Teresa of Jesus; Interior Castle; The Way of Perfection*, by St. Teresa of Avila. *Story of a Soul*, by St. Thérèse of Lisieux. *Dark Night of the Soul*, by St. John of the Cross. *The Impact of God*, by Fr. Iain Matthews. *Ascent to Love, the Spiritual Teaching of St. John of the Cross*, by Ruth Burrows. *The Dark Night of the Soul, a Psychiatrist Explores the Connection between Darkness and Spiritual Growth*, by Gerald May. *Revelations of Divine Love (Showings)*, by Julian of Norwich. *The Cloud of Unknowing*, by Anonymous. *The Practice of the Presence of God*, by Brother Lawrence. *The Way of a Pilgrim and the Pilgrim Continues His Way*, by Anonymous. *The Imitation of Christ*, by Thomas a Kempis. *Seven Storey Mountain* and *Wisdom of the Desert*, by Thomas Merton. *Practical Mysticism*, by Evelyn Underhill. *The Golden String*, by Bede Griffiths. *Prayer*, by Swami Abhishiktananda. *St. Athanasius: Life of St. Anthony*, by Athanasius. *The Rule of St. Benedict*, by St. Benedict. *Open Mind, Open Heart: The Contemplative Dimension of God*, by Thomas Keating. *Son of Man: The Mystical Path to Christ*, by Andrew Harvey. *Wisdom Distilled from the Daily: Living the Rule of*

St. Benedict, by Joan Chittister. *Searching for God*, by Cardinal Basil Hume. *The Sabbath*, by Abraham Joshua Heschel. *The Cloister Walk* and *Amazing Grace, A Vocabulary of Faith*, by Kathleen Norris. *The Way to Love, Meditations for Life*, by Anthony de Mello. *The Return of the Prodigal Son, a Spiritual Homecoming*, by Henri Neuwen. *Mere Christianity*, by C.S. Lewis. *Meeting Jesus Again for the First Time: The Historical Jesus and the Heart of Contemporary Faith*, by Marcus Borg. *The Gift*, by Hafiz. *The Essential Rumi*, by Jalal al-Din Rumi. *When Things Fall Apart* and *The Places that Scare You*, by Pema Chodron. *Peace is Every Step: The Path of Mindfulness in Everyday Life*, by Thich Nhat Hanh. *Jesus and Buddha: The Parallel Sayings*, by Marcus Borg and Jack Kornfield.

Whenever someone asks me, "What do you believe?" I'm tempted to say, "Read Richard Rohr: I think everything he thinks." Which is not quite true; if it were true, I'd be much, much wiser. But I was wise enough to absorb some of Fr. Rohr's ideas, which then came to permeate this book. Of Rohr's many excellent books, I'm most indebted to *Things Hidden, Scripture as Spirituality*, and *Job and the Mystery of Suffering*.